# FACING GOLIATH

How to Triumph in the
Dangerous Market Ahead

# FACING GOLIATH

## How to Triumph in the Dangerous Market Ahead

## KEITH SPRINGER

iUniverse, Inc.
Bloomington

# Facing Goliath
## How to Triumph in the Dangerous Market Ahead

*iUniverse books may be ordered through booksellers or by contacting:*

*iUniverse*
*1663 Liberty Drive*
*Bloomington, IN 47403*
*www.iuniverse.com*
*1-800-Authors (1-800-288-4677)*

*ISBN: 978-1-4620-0210-8 (pbk)*
*ISBN: 978-1-4620-0211-5 (ebk)*

*Printed in the United States of America*

*iUniverse rev. date: 07/23/2011*

For my son Josh, who just might someday decide to come into the family business.

# Preface

*If you can't explain what you're thinking or doing in plain English, you're probably doing something wrong!*

Have you ever read a book, report, white paper or anything related to finance, and thought to yourself *"What the hell is this guy talking about?"* or *"What a pompous windbag!"*?

Well I have, and I hate it. For some reason the authors of many investment books feel like they have to impress you with either the length of their words or the number of pages.

Not me, and not this book. I have been told that I have an ability for making even the most complicated subjects easy to understand. That's what made me get off my butt and write this book. People deserve to read in *plain English* what is happening in our economy and what to do with their money, and that's what I've tried to deliver.

Don't get me wrong, it covers a lot of information on very complicated issues. The complexity of some of the subject matter might make you scratch your head a few times (or perhaps curse under your breath in the chapters on tax policy). However, on the whole, I think you'll find it interesting, useful and—most importantly—easy to follow. I hope you enjoy reading it as much as I enjoyed writing it.

# Acknowledgements

I wish to thank my parents, for just about everything, my sister Andrea for being such a brat when we were kids that she drove me to success, Charles Sizemore who was indispensible on this project, Becky and my tremendous office staff who kept me driven and focused, Jane for her support and great cooking, Ripto for keeping me sane and Carrie for keeping me in the loop.

# Table of Contents

# Introduction

Arenal, Costa Rica—It is Monday, October 6, 2008 and the world as I know it has ended. I've just arrived at my hotel, bleary-eyed after a long red-eye flight. I have no idea what time it is. The iPhone says 6 a.m., but there is no one to be seen, not even a waiter. What I wouldn't do for a cup of coffee right about now. So much for getting away for a much needed holiday.

You might ask *why* I was frantically searching for a WiFi Internet connection in a Latin American resort hours before the business day normally started. To answer that, we have to go back in time a couple weeks. We're in the middle of the most tumultuous period the stock market has seen since the Great Depression. Just three weeks before, the unthinkable had happened: Lehman Brothers, the 158-year-old stalwart of the financial world had collapsed and declared bankruptcy. I must admit that weekend had been one of the most electrifying times in my 25+ years as a wealth advisor, and I remember that Sunday morning of September 14th as if it were yesterday. I was entertaining friends in the backyard and was a rude host that day, running back and forth from my computer to my guests, wondering who—if anyone— was going to rescue Lehman.

Sometime that afternoon, I was taken aback by news that I simply wouldn't have believed a year earlier. Merrill Lynch was in talks to be bought out by Bank of America. That could only mean one thing: they were going down, right then and there, and the immediacy indicated they couldn't open for business on Monday. They lacked the funds to continue operations. I was literally shaking with both horror and excitement, as if expecting a visit from an evil Santa Claus. My career had started with Merrill in 1985, and since then I had thought of

Merrill as being invincible. Frankly, watching it collapse was terrifying. It shattered many of the remaining illusions that I had carried with me from those early days. What a different world it was when I started. Ronald Reagan was president, the Dow was just about to cross 1,300 and the biggest bull market in world history was in its infancy.

I had believed that the worst was behind us and that I could get away for a nice holiday to clear my head. This trip to Costa Rica had been planned for almost two years, and now would be a good time to get away. Boy, was I wrong. As I awaited that cup of coffee from Juan, an attentive waiter in the Arenal Volcano Hotel lobby, I flipped on my laptop and once again felt that twisting sensation in the pit of my stomach. The Dow was down some 800 points! Oh my God, that meteor that I thought had veered from its course was now once again hurtling towards earth, only this time it was closer than ever. We hadn't avoided Armageddon; it was happening before my very eyes!

With the beautiful, vast and serene Arenal Volcano to one side and the mushroom cloud emanating from my computer on the other, I couldn't help but notice the eerie difference between the tranquility of my surroundings and the sense of panic and hysteria over the impending destruction of the world's financial foundation. It was surreal and felt something like being snatched from your mother's arms as a child and thrown to the wolves.

The world was crumbling, the financial world at least, and although I had expected such a decline eventually and was confident that I was prepared, I kept thinking that there must be more that I should have done. I had written my *Economic Tsunami* report detailing how the economy would unravel just a few months before, but I must admit that the timing caught me by surprise. Knowing that calamity is coming and living through it are two entirely different things.

Months before I had witnessed the unthinkable: the collapse of Bear Stearns, one of the biggest and baddest investment banks on the planet. They had been considered more than solvent just a few days before. But as the bank's counterparties suddenly lost faith in its ability to honor its commitments, the government was forced to broker a deal whereby JP Morgan Chase would absorb Bear. Just like that, a major Wall Street institution—a former pillar of strength and stability—went up in a puff of smoke. If it could happen to them, it could happen to anyone. Little did we know that Bear's collapse would set off a chain reaction that would eventually bring the international financial system—and global capitalism itself—to the brink of destruction in October 2008.

And so that is how I found myself in a hotel lobby that morning, attempting to deal with the implications of this meltdown for my clients from the wilds of Costa Rica. Over the several tense days that followed, I did my best to calm client fears while continuously reevaluating my strategy to not only protect my clients' money but to take advantage of the situation. After all, people weren't paying me to sit like a deer in the headlights. As a wealth advisor, I am expected to actually make money.

To keep my head clear, I managed to toss in a little adventure: zip-lining through the Monteverde rain forest, repelling through the 100 ft. Fortuna waterfalls and rafting down the class 4 and 5 rapids of the Toro River with the Howler monkeys, well, howling at the top of their lungs. It was as though they were laughing at me and my feeble attempt to escape reality, if even for just a moment. I must admit, had it not been for such audacious activities that instill the fear of death in you, I would have probably gone insane.

I managed to unwind a little by enjoying some of the excellent locally made cigars during the daily afternoon downpours, giving me time to ponder. I was fortunate enough to have had a private tour of Don Benigno's cigar factory at the beginning of our trip, highlighted by a visit from Don Benigno himself. He had a trick he liked to show off where he would stand one of his cigars on its ash. Because Don Benigo's cigars are rolled so perfectly, they would stand up on their own!

As we sat in his courtyard, sipping espresso and enjoying his finest Robusto while trying desperately to understand each other in my broken Spanish, I couldn't help but feel jealous at his innocent obliviousness to the meteor that was hurtling towards earth and mere seconds from impact.

I managed to finish my wonderful journey after scuba diving with the hammerheads off Cocos Island, while racking up a satellite phone bill the size of a mortgage payment. Although sad at the end of my trip, I needed to be home to witness the carnage for myself and to at least have the feeling of being in control again. As I finally got off the plane in Sacramento, I half expected to see people screaming, buildings burning and smoke billowing from the sky. Of course that's not what was going on at all. The "real" world appeared to be completely unconcerned about the precarious cracks in the foundation of our financial system. It would be several months until the average man on the street would feel the effects. Lucky stiff!

I realized a very important reality that month: **The laws for investing had changed.** No longer could you just buy a mutual fund and sit back and watch it go up like we did in the 80s and 90s. No longer could we buy the stock of a household name and hold it forever like our grandparents did. No, buy-and-hold was dead, having turned into *buy-and-hope*. For the foreseeable future, to be successful one would have to take a tactical approach.

As a wealth manager, I am conservative by design. I don't swing for the fences or put people in a "one size fits all" investment package. My holistic approach is distinctive in the industry, identifying not just clients' financial goals but their *life's* goals. Most of all, I believe in managing my clients' money in a very structured and disciplined way in order to get the very best returns with the least risk possible. Typically, I strive to get 70-80% of the upside of the market while only taking 20-30% of the downside.

Back in December 2007, well before the catastrophe I describe above, I wrote my landmark report: *An Economic Tsunami Lies Ahead – How to Prepare for This Perfect Storm,* which forecasted such a calamity. In the late 1990s, I began studying the effects that demographics have on the economy and on the markets. It became clear that economies grow when there are a lot of people entering their peak spending years of life, and they slow when people get older and prepare for retirement.

I soon recognized that our population was aging fast, and within a few years the largest segment of our population, the Baby Boomers, would be past their peak spending years. This alone was a disaster waiting to happen. However, when I realized that our nation's personal debt levels had skyrocketed to a point that was unsustainable, largely because we were using credit as a substitute for actual buyers, I knew we were facing no ordinary challenge. For the average investor confronting violent forces of such magnitude—like David standing toe-to-toe with a towering, muscle-bound Goliath—the odds looked very bleak indeed.

Although I had largely prepared my clients for the event, the meltdown was a devastating end to one of the worst decades in the history of the U.S. stock market, which begs the question:

"Where do we go from here?"

If there is one question I hear most from my clients in the wake of the ordeal, this is it. After a lost decade for investors with not one but two bear markets, a housing collapse and the most severe credit crisis since 1907—a true once-in-a-hundred-years' event—people are angry, scared and more than a little frustrated. There is a pervading sense of fear and anxiety in the air. In my 25+ years in this business, I have never seen people as uneasy about the future as they are today.

Investors are right to be concerned. At the time of writing, the S&P 500 index is trading near 1,200, a level that it first reached in 1998. This means that buy-and-hold investors or those holding an S&P 500 index fund or similar investment have seen no return on their investments in over 12 years, excluding dividend income (Figure 0.1).

Figure 0.1: S&P 500 Index

A lost decade in the stock market

Source: Bloomberg

Twelve years is a ridiculously long time to go without a positive return. Some advisors, brokers, and bankers have the gall to say that it's ok, because "over the long run, the market always goes up," or, "the crash happened to everyone and you should just ride it out." Not me. That's just plain lunacy. Even worse for these poor schmucks is that this lost decade happened at a devastating time for investors in the peak earning years of their late 40s and 50s. Retirement for many of these investors depended on their ability to earn respectable returns during those crucial years. Today, many have had to postpone retirement indefinitely or to accept a retirement lifestyle far more modest than they had planned. Dreams of sailing around the world or simply spending more time with the grandkids would have to remain dreams. Many will even have to work for the rest of their lives.

Of course, many Americans have a significant portion of their wealth tied up in the equity in their home. The model for prior generations was to sell their large suburban homes that had appreciated in value over the years and to use the proceeds to help fund a comfortable retirement. A retiring couple could sell their suburban home for, say, $500,000, whereas the new retirement home might only cost $250,000. The difference could be used to fund an annuity. At current market rates, $250,000 would generate roughly $1,200 per month to a hypothetical husband and wife aged 62. Many would-be retirees had budgeted this income to supplement Social Security and their other pensions and investments. With the prices of homes down significantly in most American cities and with home equity decimated as a result, this is no longer a viable option.

Meanwhile, the depth of the recession and the aggressiveness of the federal government's response have caused government debt to spiral out of control, rivaling that of a banana republic. Currently, the total federal debt stands at a whopping $13 trillion. Debts, of course, have to be repaid. And in the private sector, we are starting to see this. Total debt outstanding by individuals and corporations is actually shrinking (Figure 0.2). In fact, the private sector is paying off debts faster than the government is accruing them. Though this process of deleveraging is essential to the long-term health of the country, it comes at a heavy cost. Every dollar used to repay debt is a dollar that cannot be spent in the economy.

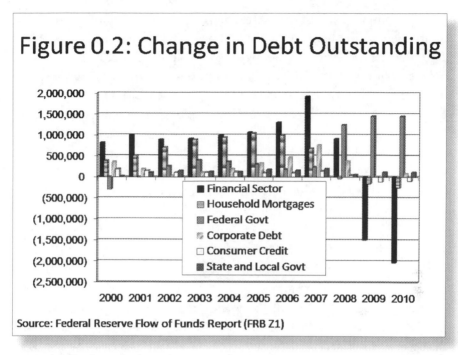

Figure 0.2: Change in Debt Outstanding

Legend:
- Financial Sector
- Household Mortgages
- Federal Govt
- Corporate Debt
- Consumer Credit
- State and Local Govt

Source: Federal Reserve Flow of Funds Report (FRB Z1)

What is done is done. We cannot change the past, and the question remains "Where do we go from here?"

This is the question I intend to answer in the pages that follow, and the outlook is mixed.

There is good news and there is bad news. The good news is that after reading this book, you will be prepared. The bad news is that the excesses of the past twenty years will take time to get worked off. In America's borrowing binge, private-sector and government debts simply got out of control. Debt is a way of bringing future consumption into the present. A dollar borrowed to use today is a dollar that is unavailable to be spent tomorrow. That is, unless you intend to borrow another dollar. Of course, there are limits to the amount of borrowing that can be done. Americans learned this the hard way in 2008 and 2009 when the entire credit system came crashing down. As a result, the next several years will be marked by Americans paying down their debts. The result, to the surprise of many, absent government intervention through stimulus, will likely be a prolonged period of deflation or at the very least extremely low inflation.

As I mentioned briefly, demographics plays a large role here. The

Baby Boomer generation has reached a critical threshold. The bulk of the generation has now passed its peak years for spending growth. They have now reached the stage of their lives marked by saving, not spending. As the biggest and richest generation in history, this retrenchment by the Boomers will be a major headwind for the U.S. economy. This is a line of research and analysis that was pioneered by Harry S Dent, Jr. Harry's contribution to the industry's understanding of how demographics impact the economy has been immeasurable and his research served as a cornerstone of this work.

The good news is that despite the precarious state of the economy, there are positive trends that we can follow. The Echo Boomers, the kids of the original Baby Boomers, are now entering the family-formation stage themselves. They will one day enter their peak spending stages of life and create the next wave of aggregate demand the economy needs. That day unfortunately is not today, or even tomorrow but several years out. Not until this generation emerges *en force* will the next durable bull market begin. Even amid the gloom of 2008 and 2009, the American birth rate remained at levels not seen since the 1960s. Given that the majority of Echo Boomers has yet to marry and start families—and therefore enter their peak spending years—I see this as a trend that is likely to last for several years to come. These new American families represent the future for the country, and the future will indeed be bright—once we get through the current hell to pay from previous excesses.

Outside of the United States, we are witnessing economic miracles happening in the emerging market countries of Asia and Latin America. Millions of people who formerly toiled as low-wage laborers are entering the new global middle class every year. The emergence of this new middle class is the single biggest growth story of the next twenty years.

Even in the crisis-plagued United States, great opportunities exist for investors to repair their balance sheets and fund their retirements. Many of America's best companies are trading at bargain prices and pay cash dividends that are higher than 30-year bond yields. Even during a prolonged economic slump, a portfolio of high-yielding blue chips with a proven track record of surviving and prospering in difficult conditions offer the potential for respectable returns. However, as you will learn, it's not always the obvious blue chips with their mediocre dividends that provide the best success, but identifying that niche marketplace of undervalued stocks that pay extraordinary dividends.

Investors can also find value in relatively new sectors, such as master limited partnerships (MLPs). Given that bonds do not yield enough to fund the income needs of most investors, MLPs—which often yield 8–10% or more—can be a nice addition to a portfolio. MLP yields—like stock dividends but unlike bond coupon payments—also tend to rise over time.

Preferred stock is another good option for generating income. Preferred stock is a security that offers some of the best aspects of both stocks and bonds. Like bonds, the emphasis of preferred stock is on the cash yield it pays. Preferred stock often pays substantially higher yields than comparable bonds, however, while also remaining considerably less volatile than regular common stocks.

In short, we are looking at several difficult years ahead. But with proper planning and tactical portfolio management, this is not something that should concern us. Uncertainty creates opportunity. As my good friend Tom once said, "Never let a good crisis go to waste!"

In the pages that follow, I intend to explain how we arrived at where we are today and how we as investors can prosper, regardless of which direction the economy takes.

# Chapter 1:

# How Did We Get Here?

Unless you've spent the last few years in a cave, you know very well: it's rough out there.

Home prices nationwide peaked in early 2006 and have been declining ever since with no end in sight. The unemployment rate stubbornly continues to hover near the 10% mark, the highest levels since the 1982 recession (see Figures 1.1 and 1.2). The FDIC continues to shut down insolvent banks. And perhaps most ominously, a debilitating sense of gloom and despair pervades the country.

In times like this, it is fair to ask: **What the hell happened?**

Those readers familiar with the legal system have no doubt heard the expression "proximate cause." It tends to come up most frequently in lawsuits. The proximate cause is the cause closest to an event. There may have been plenty of contributing factors along the way, but the proximate cause is the last one.

The proximate cause for the Great Recession was the credit crisis that began in late 2007 when the banks first began to acknowledge their losses on their subprime mortgage portfolios. The crisis accelerated in 2008 with the failures of Bear Stearns and Lehman Brothers. By the time the crisis abated in early 2009, the damage was done. The credit system was impaired, Americans collectively lost hundreds of billions of dollars of accumulated wealth, and consumer confidence was shattered.

## Figure 1.1: Case Shiller 20-City Home Price Index

Source: Standard & Poor's

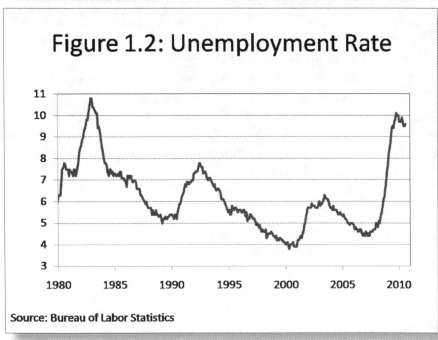

## Figure 1.2: Unemployment Rate

Source: Bureau of Labor Statistics

Fast forward to today and not much fundamentally has changed. A steady stream of government stimulus has at least given the illusion of stability, and Americans are no longer paralyzed by anxiety—yet they are not exactly oozing confidence either. They are starting to spend money again, slowly and in fits and starts. But the old swagger is long gone, as is the willingness to take risk.

A bona fide credit crisis is a crisis of confidence that results in a destabilizing lack of liquidity. But in layman's terms what does that actually *mean*? Where does the liquidity "go" at the onset of a crisis? After all, can money just disappear?

In the bank runs of the 1800s and early 1900s, the mechanics were fairly simple. For any number of reasons, real or imagined, depositors would lose faith in a bank as the steward of their savings and would demand their money back—in cold, hard cash. Of course, banks only keep a small fraction of customer deposits on hand and loan out the rest. So, when demand for deposited funds exceeds the cash on hand, the bank is forced to call in loans, and the borrowers have to scramble to find other sources of funding. Otherwise, they have to liquidate their assets in order to pay back their debts. Of course, buyers for those assets would be scarce because the financing to make a sale possible would be unavailable—after all, if the bank is calling in existing loans, it doesn't have the cash on hand to facilitate the deal. The result is a downward spiral of fear and panic and, typically, a severe bear market, recession and downward pressure on prices.

The Federal Reserve was created in 1913 to prevent these kinds of bank runs. Going forward, banks would have the ability to take short-term borrowings from the Fed in order to satisfy immediate liquidity needs. In other words, the Fed can act like a giant pawn shop, offering emergency loans as needed. And like a pawn shop might take your watch as a security deposit, the Fed takes high-quality bonds from the borrowing bank's portfolio as collateral for the loan.

Furthermore, by regulating the Fed funds rate, the Fed can lower the cost of funds for short-term loans between banks. Lowering the Fed funds rate had the effect of injecting liquidity into the system. Banks had no reason to fear systemic collapse and could thus lend freely to one another. We could all have confidence in the system.

So what went wrong in 2007 and 2008? Why, for all intents and purposes, did we have an old-school crisis of confidence? Where did the liquidity go?

For answers, we turn to Paul McCulley, Managing Director of Pimco, the world's largest bond management firm. Writing for the CFA Institute, Mr. McCulley says:

> My simple thesis is that **liquidity is a state of mind**. In the current market and talk of a liquidity crunch, investors are asking, where did the liquidity go? This question reflects the concept taught in basic economics that the money stock is the liquidity in the market, which creates the concept of liquidity as a pool of money. It is a very bank-centric concept of liquidity; the U.S. Federal Reserve (Fed) injects and withdraws liquidity, and the banks transform liquidity into deposits and loans. Thus, investors think of liquidity as a pool of money, and during a downturn, they wonder where the liquidity went.
>
> **My answer is that liquidity is not a fixed pool of money but, rather, a state of mind and, in particular, a state of mind regarding risk.** Liquidity is the result of the appetite of investors to underwrite risk and the appetite of savers to provide leverage to investors who want to underwrite risk. **The greater the risk appetite, the greater the liquidity**, and vice versa. Put another way, liquidity is the joining or separating of two states of mind—a leveraged investor who wants to underwrite risk and an unleveraged saver who does not want to take risk and who is the source of liquidity to the levered investor. The alignment or misalignment of the two investors determines the abundance or shortage of liquidity.[1]

Therefore, what we had here was a good old fashioned crisis of confidence, and there is no telling when a crisis will rear its ugly head. When it starts there is no stopping it. Panic and fear will always prevail over rational behavior.

Financial markets and the capitalist economy are driven by what John Maynard Keynes called "animal spirits," which, if you have ever seen the hyperactive trading floor of the New York Stock Exchange, needs no further explanation. Unfortunately, the instinct that drives these animal spirits can quickly turn to fear, which has largely been the case since 2007.

Speculative booms generally end in deflationary busts, and the epicenter of the speculation typically endures a long period of contraction and stagnation as the excesses of the boom are slowly absorbed and worked off. In the case of the subprime mortgage crisis, a speculative house of cards was built around a single premise: that home prices would always rise, thus making mortgage lending (even subprime, ARMs, "no doc", etc.) a near riskless business, particularly if mortgages were properly bundled to diversify the risk.

There is a demographic story here as well. The boom in housing that made all of this possible was a result of the Baby Boomer trade-up cycle, in which successful Boomers used their hard-earned spending power to buy the homes of their dreams. Once the boom reached the speculative bubble stage, the buying spread far beyond the financially sound core of middle-class Boomers to lower-income and younger marginal buyers. Finally, when mania set in, would-be homeowners were afraid of being left behind by their peers if they *didn't* buy. After they watched their home-owning neighbors score enormous paper gains on their properties, they felt, in the desperate logic that dominates a mania, that they couldn't afford *not* to buy.

When adjustable rate mortgages began to reset and marginal buyers were unable to continue paying or to refinance at the then-prevailing mortgage rate, the default rate on mortgages started to soar. Furthermore, the higher interest rates caused the value of virtually all long-term bonds to fall, included mortgage bonds and the alphabet soup of derivatives based on them (MBS, CMS, etc.) As homes and the mortgages written on those homes continued to fall in value, no bank or broker was willing to accept mortgage bonds on derivatives as collateral for new loans. It would be like going to a pawn shop for business as usual and discovering that the pawnshop owner abruptly stopped accepting watches like the one you intended to pawn as collateral.

When "Bank A" gets scared and refuses to accept the bonds as collateral, "Bank B" gets scared too and follows suit. Suddenly, there are no takers in the marketplace. The watch on your wrist, whether a Rolex or a Timex, is suddenly viewed as worthless trash that no pawnbroker would lend against.

The Rolex/Timex analogy is crude but not altogether inaccurate. During much of the credit crunch, legitimate AAA-rated assets (the "Rolexes") were shunned almost as much as the subprime toxic waste (the "Timexes"). A case in point was the sad end of Thornburg Mortgage. Thornburg's business consisted of making jumbo mortgages to wealthy "superprime" borrowers buying expensive homes with jumbo mortgages. That's *super*prime—as in *better* than prime—not *sub*prime, meaning that these were the absolute best of the best of mortgage borrowers. Thornburg was selling Rolexes, not Timexes. Nevertheless, the company quickly found its financing cutoff and was eventually forced into bankruptcy due to margin calls.

This brings up another arcane term that wreaked havoc during the crisis: "mark to market." Hedge funds, investment banks, and lenders like Thornburg have to carry the assets (mortgage loans) on their books at "fair market value," meaning the prevailing price. The problem is, when there are no buyers, there is no market price to be marked to, and so the price drops precipitously. Suddenly, the mortgage assets held in these companies' portfolios are worth considerably less or nothing at all, but the money that they borrowed to fund those assets still has to be paid back. In many cases, these "mark to market" losses might only be temporary. But that doesn't stop, say, a company like Thornburg Mortgage, from being in technical default and from being forced to sell assets at a fire-sale price in order to meet short-term liabilities. This further reduces the price, which causes more fire-sale selling from others, causing the downward spiral that we witnessed during the crisis. So where does it all end?

The move by the Federal Reserve to accept "nontraditional" collateral on loans (e.g., mortgage assets) and to massively expand its balance sheet to unprecedented levels was an attempt to put a backstop in place (see Figure 1.3). It had the desired effect of alleviating the immediate state of crisis. It did *not*, however, mean that we would return to business as usual. As McCulley noted in the quote above, this crisis was not due to a lack of cash in the system. In a money system like ours, there can never be a lack of cash because cash can be "printed" at will. And the Fed did quite a bit of that, as Figure 1.4 makes abundantly clear. The adjusted monetary base, the foundation on which the money supply is built, was more than doubled by Fed Chairman Ben Bernanke's aggressive open-market operation.

To create "new" money, the Fed buys existing bonds from their owners for cash. This monetizing of the debt is the modern equivalent of "priming the printing presses." One might have expected hyperinflation to result from such a surge, but instead prices fell. I'll get into the mechanics of why this happened in the following chapters. For now, suffice it to say that there was no inflation because the new money never actually entered the financial system. The banks were too scared to lend it out, and few consumers or businesses were interested in borrowing.

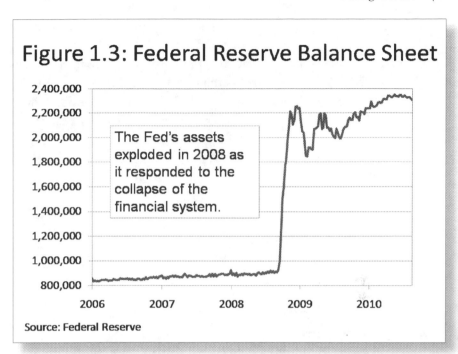

# Figure 1.3: Federal Reserve Balance Sheet

The Fed's assets exploded in 2008 as it responded to the collapse of the financial system.

Source: Federal Reserve

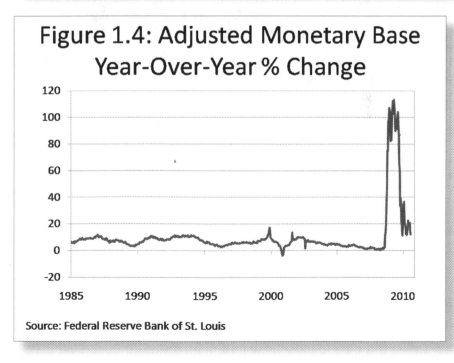

# Figure 1.4: Adjusted Monetary Base Year-Over-Year % Change

Source: Federal Reserve Bank of St. Louis

I believe that we are in the early stages of a Japanese "Lost Decades" scenario in which the pace of economic activity slows down. Interest rates fall, but low rates do not have the stimulative effect that they used to. Monetary policy fails to work its magic and becomes analogous to "pushing on a string." Fiscal policy (a.k.a. taxing and spending) fails to spur the economy as well. Consumers become more conservative: they spend less on virtually everything and save more. They are less interested in borrowing from banks and less interested in loaning or investing their money in the form of speculative bonds and stocks. Banks and other investors are generally not in a position to be as generous in making loans because their balance sheets are still in need of repair after the excesses of the boom.

Many of the major financial powerhouses have recently had to "recapitalize" by issuing new stock or convertible debt to investors, with Citigroup being one of the highest-profile cases. Needless to say, the new Citi is going to be a little more risk averse than in years past. Credit will not be issued as freely.

It appears the government recognizes this, at least to a minor extent, as the massive "quantitative easing" programs are simply helping the banks repair their balance sheets and are doing little for middle America. It seems to me that they are preparing for big trouble, perhaps a scuffle with Goliath, and they want the banks in a better position next time.

In any event, the end result will be a long-term slowing in which there is less overall economic activity. Welcome to Japan, circa 1990.

I'll write at length about Japan and its economic malaise of the past two decades in a later chapter. But first, I want to make my case for why it is deflation—not inflation—that I see in the immediate future, and I will tell you what this means for your life and your investment.

# Chapter 2:

# Inflation or Deflation Ahead?

Naturally, we all would like to pay less for the things we buy. So, wouldn't a period of deflation, in which the price of virtually everything falls, be good for consumers?

As it turns out, there is both good deflation and bad deflation. When a breakthrough in technology lowers the price of inputs, the producer can sell the finished good to the consumer at a lower price and still make a reasonable profit. For example, if Intel discovers a way to make its processor chips cheaper, Dell Computer can pay less for those chips and then pass on the savings to the consumer in the form of cheaper computers. Some readers might have heard of "Moore's Law," named after Gordon Moore, co-founder of Intel. Moore's Law states that computing power roughly doubles every two years. Meanwhile, prices on computers continue to fall. More computational power for less money is a win for everyone. That's good deflation.

The discovery of a major oil field could lower the cost of crude oil and ultimately retail gasoline. Again, everyone benefits. Unfortunately, we also have "bad deflation," which is created from a contraction in demand, not a surge in supply.

Now, I'm going to get a little technical here, but there's no better way to say it. Consider Figure 2.1. S1 is the supply curve, which represents the volume of output that producers are willing and able to produce at each price. The line has a positive slope, which makes sense. Apple has a greater incentive to crank out a higher volume of iPhones when the price is higher rather than lower.

## Figure 2.1: An Economy at Equilibrium

The consumer has the exact opposite motivations, as illustrated by D1, the demand curve. At lower prices, consumers are willing to buy more. In a given family budget, there might be enough cash for one $70 Polo shirt. But if Polo lowered the price to $10, the family has enough cash in the budget for seven shirts. Along the same lines, you might be more tempted to buy an extra Big Mac at McDonalds when they run a 99-cent special than when then charge full price. The key here is that, in general, a *decrease* in the price means an *increase* in the volume sold, and vice versa.

The point at which supply and demand intersect is the equilibrium price, the "normal" price that satisfies both the buyer and the seller. Any deviation from this equilibrium price will result in short-term shortages or surpluses. Those $10 Polo shirts are not likely to stay on the racks very long, and 99-cent Big Macs are likely to be eaten quickly—creating shortages. But that same shirt at $150 is likely to stay on the rack a lot longer, and a Big Mac priced at $10 is likely to stay under the heat lamp—creating surpluses.

Now, let us consider a situation whereby a new technological breakthrough massively reduces the cost of production, enabling companies to increase their output while simultaneously lowering their prices. This is illustrated by Figure 2.2, Supply-Based "Good Deflation."

Figure 2.2: Supply-Based "Good" Deflation

When a new technological breakthrough pushes the supply curve out, prices fall while unit production rises.

Figure 2.3: Demand-Based "Bad" Deflation

When an external event like a credit crisis reduces the ability to finance consumption, prices and unit production fall

As S1 is pushed out to S2, the price falls and the output rises. This has been the general trend for manufactured products since the dawn of the Industrial Revolution, and the result has been an incredible increase in real incomes and a massive improvement in the standard of living for the human race. The computer that is being used to write this book is exponentially more powerful than the ones used just ten years ago, and it cost a fraction of the price. Computers purchased a few years from today will no doubt be exponentially more powerful than this one, and—again—a fraction of the price. This is the deflation of technological progress and productivity, and it is certainly nothing to worry about over the long term.

Technological improvements *do* wreak havoc on existing producers, of course. For example, the advent of mobile phones and Internet telephony providers like Vonage and Skype flooded the market with cheap communications tools, which caused prices to plummet. This has rendered the legacy operations of phone companies like Verizon obsolete, and the fixed line business is slowly dying as a result. However, the benefits to society of lower communications costs far outweigh any negatives from the decline of the traditional phone companies. The increases in communication and productivity are major net positives.

In Figure 2.3, however, we see plenty to worry about. It shows what is happening today in the housing market and in the retail economy. Supply remains steady but the demand curve is pushed back. The result is both a lower price *and* lower quantity. No one wins here.

This is the key difference between good and bad deflation. In good deflation, demand remains strong and unit output increases, sometimes substantially. Profits thus can grow and companies can expand and hire new workers even as prices fall. In bad deflation, output falls and companies often are forced to shut stores or factories and to lay off workers. The auto industry is a case in point here. Facing relentless competition from stronger foreign rivals, the Big Three found themselves with a hopeless amount of excess capacity. When demand began to fall in late 2008 due to rising fuel costs and a dysfunctional credit system, they had to slash prices and offer incentives, and they still had trouble moving the metal. Before the dust settled, both General Motors and Chrysler were bankrupt and Ford just barely escaped the same fate.

What Happened?

In the case of good deflation, we know that technology and productivity are the causes. But in the current crisis, what is driving the deflationary forces? Why has the demand curve been pulled back?

The answer is simple. There are two primary components to consumer behavior: the *willingness* to spend and the *ability* to spend. Demographics are perhaps the largest contributing factor in the willingness and desire to consume, and this is a topic I'll return to in a later chapter. For now, just remember that demographic factors like age and stage of life are the primary motivators in most consumer spending decisions.

Of course, in order to actually make purchases, a consumer must have cash. Or credit.

During the recession of the early 2000s following the tech bust, free-flowing credit allowed consumers to continue spending. Strong demographic trends ensured they did exactly that. The result was a relatively mild and short-lived downturn.

This time around, the situation was fundamentally different. The collapse of the financial sector had the effect of pulling the rug out from under both the consumer and business sectors. Suddenly, consumers found themselves unable to refinance their homes to "extract equity." The home refinancing boom of the mid-2000s was a significant provider of consumer spending power that has now been effectively shut down. What bank would be reckless enough to refinance a mortgage that is now under water due to the decline in home prices?

Meanwhile, businesses too found themselves unable to roll over their loans. Thornburg Mortgage, which I mentioned in the last chapter, was a high-profile victim of the collapse of the auction rate securities market. Unable to secure regular financing, the company found itself having to sell assets in an illiquid market to avoid default. Thornburg was ruined, delisted from the New York Stock Exchange and eventually had to file for bankruptcy protection.

Even the venerable General Electric found itself having to turn to Warren Buffett, hat in hand, for financing. Mr. Buffett obliged, but he took the proverbial pound of flesh in return. General Electric, a AAA-rated company at the time, agreed to pay Buffett's Berkshire

Hathaway 10% on the preferred stock issue and even issued warrants (stock options) as a sweetener.

The result for both consumers and businesses has been a stampede to "deleverage," paying down existing debts and putting large new purchases on hold. With each marginal dollar being used to pay down existing debts rather than fund new consumption, the demand curve in Figure 2.3 has been rather violently wrenched backward, taking prices down in the process.

Also, a profound psychological change accompanies the deflationary environment. The public mood and popular media in the U.S. reflect a new reality. Splurging is as outmoded as the Hummer. Bargains are the new black. In 2009, the media abounded with advice on "cool" ways to save money. Suddenly, clipping coupons was a sign of respectability! Newspaper reviews of fine cuisine gave way to hackneyed features about "comfort food." Home improvement TV programming switched from house-flipping to *Income Property*, and late-night infomercials began counseling how to sell your belongings on eBay to raise cash.

## Why is This a Problem?

The psychological aspect is perhaps the scariest part. The fear of deflation can become a self-fulfilling prophecy, and when it does, economic activity grinds to a halt. As unpleasant as inflation is, it is the fear of deflation that keeps Fed chairmen awake at night. Before taking the job, Ben Bernanke was known infamously as "Helicopter Ben" for comments made about deflation. To paraphrase, Mr. Bernanke said, only half joking, that the Federal Reserve would do anything in its power to avoid deflation, even if it meant literally dumping dollars out of helicopters in the hopes that someone would spend them.

It is also worth mentioning that when Franklin Delano Roosevelt famously said *"The only thing we have to fear is fear itself,"* he referred not to the Nazi regime or of looming war. No, Roosevelt meant the vicious cycle of pessimism brought on by deflation, which he went on to call a "nameless, unreasoning, unjustified terror which paralyzes needed efforts to convert retreat into advance."

What Now?

We currently have too much capacity virtually everywhere (Figure 2.4), which means pricing power is all but nonexistent. Capacity utilization measures what percentage of our production capacity is currently being used. As you can see, it had rebounded from the pits of late 2009, but even after the recovery it is barely higher that it was during the *lows* of the early 2000s recession.

Demographic trends suggest that these conditions can linger far longer than most economists think. As the Baby Boomers accelerate the downsizing of their lives in preparation for retirement, aggregate demand will be sorely lacking in the economy. These conditions still linger in Japan, nearly 20 years after the Japanese stock and property bubbles reached their explosive peaks and collapsed.

## Figure 2.4: Capacity Utilization

Source: Federal Reserve

President Obama, like Former President Bush, understands the dangers of deflation and is attempting to "legislate" inflation through federal fiscal stimulus. As illustrated in Figure 2.5, the president hopes to use tax cuts and deficit spending on infrastructure projects to push the demand curve forward, thus raising prices. At the very least, it will give the illusion that it's working while all that free money is sloshing around the economy looking for a place to go. This will simply mask the problem, rather than fix the inherent condition, creating yet another bubble. This will produce an effect similar to that of Viagra. Temporary, but good while it lasts.

Mr. Obama may be mildly successful in the short term, but his stimulus plan will not be any more effective than those undertaken in Japan during the 1990s. Besides, the popular uprising in the form of the Tea Party has already more or less guaranteed that there will be no more major direct stimulus gift plans going forward. President Obama came to office promising a "New Era of Responsibility," but the jury's out on whether we'll get it.

## Figure 2.5: Demand-Based Inflation

Are the Government's Actions Inflationary?

If you are regular readers, chances are good that you have a stake in the system. You likely either have a successful career or are retired after a lifetime of hard work. You pay your taxes, you vote, and if you are like me, you are concerned about the ballooning federal budget deficit (Figure 2.6). As individuals, we would never consistently spend more money than we make. To do so would be irresponsible. Yet this is exactly what our government does year after year, regardless of which party is in power.

In its efforts to stimulate the economy, the government has run previously unimaginable budget deficits. This deficit spending and the Fed's unprecedented monetary stimulus (see Figures 1.3 and 1.4 in the prior chapter) have many investors worried about inflation or even hyperinflation.

**Figure 2.6: U.S. Federal Budget Surplus and Deficit in $Billions**

The budget deficit exploded as the economy collapsed into recession and the government used aggressive fiscal stimulus.

Source: Congressional Budget Office

I understand the concern. According to standard monetary economics, monetizing the debt and spending beyond your means are a recipe for inflation. We are, however, living in extraordinary times.

As quickly as the federal government is racking up new debts, the private sector—and particularly the financial sector—is actually paying back its debts faster. Consider Figure 2.7. Starting in the mid-1990s, the United States went on a debt binge. The financial sector was by far the biggest offender, followed by household mortgages. Of course, much of the financial sector debt is *based* on mortgages and derivatives of mortgages via the alphabet soup of mortgage-backed securities (MBS), collateralized mortgage obligations (CMO) and the now almost ridiculous sounding CMOs of CMOs, or $CMO^2$.

So, the financial sector bubble and the housing bubble were really one in the same. And with mortgage lending currently a fraction of what it used to be and the market for new mortgage derivative securities practically nonexistent, it should come as no surprise to see the total debt in these sectors falling. Banks and individual Americans alike are paying down existing debts and are not adding new ones.

Figure 2.8, which is a repeat of Figure 0.2 from the introduction, has a way of putting the debt data in perspective. This chart shows the year-over-year change in debt by sector. As you can see, the deleveraging of the financial sector dwarfs the borrowing of the government.

Remember, in a credit-based economy, cash and debt are essentially the same thing. As the commercials remind us, "for the rest there is MasterCard." But a dollar used to pay down existing debts is a dollar that does not get spent in the economy. It is a destruction of purchasing power and an important reason why deflation, not inflation, will be with us for a long time to come. Quite simply, credit and therefore money is being destroyed faster than the government can create it!

Figure 2.7: Total Debt Outstanding

Source: Federal Reserve Flow of Funds Report (FRB Z1)

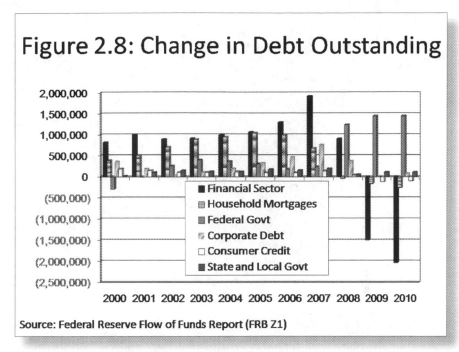

# Figure 2.8: Change in Debt Outstanding

Legend:
- Financial Sector
- Household Mortgages
- Federal Govt
- Corporate Debt
- Consumer Credit
- State and Local Govt

Years: 2000 2001 2002 2003 2004 2005 2006 2007 2008 2009 2010

Source: Federal Reserve Flow of Funds Report (FRB Z1)

If Japan's recent history is any guide—and you will soon see why it is—then the United States will likely run large budget deficits for years or even a decade or more, causing our national debt to expand to levels previously thought unimaginable. Despite this, I see overall levels of debt falling, continuing the trends of Figures 2.7 and 2.8.

As I noted earlier, in a credit-based economy, money and debt are essentially the same thing. Debts are being repaid, which is deflationary. But interestingly, the money supply is also shrinking, even as the monetary base remains outsized. Consider Figure 2.9, which tracks M3, the broadest measure of the money supply. M3 includes physical notes and coins, traveler's checks, checking accounts, savings accounts, certificates of deposits, and some forms of money market accounts.

Figure 2.9: Money Supply M3

Source: www.shadowstats.com

So, even while the monetary base has been more than doubled by the Federal Reserve since the onset of the crisis, the actual money in the real economy has shrunk.

You might be wondering how this is possible, and the answer is the fractional reserve banking system. For money to enter the financial system, it has to be loaned into existence. With credit standards higher these days, banks are less willing to lend, and consumers are less willing to borrow, particularly the aging Baby Boomers who have very little reason to borrow at this stage of their lives. As a result, the massive increase in the monetary base sits dormant in reserve in the banks' accounts at the Fed.

I've saved what is perhaps the most disturbing chart for last. Some readers might have heard the term "velocity of money" before, but most Americans have only a vague idea of what it means. It is a somewhat arcane term, but it is important in understanding what drives inflation and deflation. Money velocity is every bit as important as money supply in determining the price level.

In a nutshell, money velocity is exactly what it sounds like. It's the speed at which a dollar changes hands. Think of it this way. If Peter pays Paul a dollar for a snow cone and Paul in turn takes that same dollar and buys a Coke from Mary, there has been two dollars worth of transactions. If instead Peter buys two snow cones from Paul for a combined two dollars and then Paul simply saves the money for a rainy day rather than buy a Coke from Mary, there has also been two dollars worth of transactions. In the real economy, it does not matter if we spend multiple dollars or if we pass the same dollar around multiple times.

Perhaps it might be easier to tell it in a story:

It is a slow day in the small California town of Davis. The streets are deserted. Times are tough. Everybody is in debt and living on credit.

A tourist visiting the area drives through town, stops at the motel, and lays a $100 bill on the desk saying he wants to inspect the rooms upstairs to pick one for the night.

As soon as he walks upstairs, the motel owner grabs the bill and runs next door to pay his debt to the butcher.

The butcher takes the $100 and runs down the street to retire his debt to the pig farmer.

The pig farmer takes the $100 and heads off to pay his bill to his supplier, the Co-op.

The guy at the co-op takes the $100 and runs to pay his debt to the woman who's a vendor of the world's oldest professional service.

The woman rushes to the hotel and pays off her room bill with the hotel owner.

The hotel proprietor then places the $100 back on the counter so the traveler will not suspect anything.

At that moment the traveler comes down the stairs, states

that the rooms are not satisfactory, picks up the $100 bill and leaves.

No one produced anything. No one earned anything. However, the whole town is now out of debt and now looks to the future with a lot more optimism.

And that, ladies and gentlemen, is how money velocity works. Money velocity is hard to accurately calculate and so often ends up being a "plug" number in economics equations.[2] Still, we can approximate it by dividing GDP by the monetary base (Figure 2.10).

Figure 2.10: Velocity of Money
GDP to Adjusted Monetary Base

Source: St. Louis Fed, US BEA

In case anyone has lingering questions about why we had deflation in 2008 and 2009 rather than runaway inflation, Figure 2.10 should answer it. The pace of economic activity plummeted during the crisis and has yet to recover. The Fed made a lot of new money available, but no one seemed interested in spending it!

Without belaboring the point, in a following chapter I want to offer one final explanation for the rate of inflation or deflation: demographics. But first, I want to take a short trip across the Pacific—to Japan.

# Chapter 3:

# History Repeating Itself Across the Pacific

Mark Twain, one of America's favorite literary figures, understood the rhythms of history. Twain noted that history did not *repeat* itself, per se. Instead, it rhymes.

Events never unfold in exactly the same manner twice. There are different people involved and different sets of circumstances. But nevertheless, the stories tend to be remarkably similar. I bring this up because Japan went through a debt bubble and crisis two decades ago just like our own. It is scary how similar the two countries' situations are, and it certainly provides a sobering vision of our future.

Japan was the first modern "miracle" economy in the years following World War II. No country in history could match Japan's growth rates from the 1950s through the 1970s. In just two decades, Japan evolved from a largely agrarian country to an industrial powerhouse that rivaled the United States. By the 1980s, Americans suddenly found themselves struggling to compete with Japanese manufacturers of steel, autos and consumer electronics. The staid, conservative Swiss watch industry was decimated by upstarts like Japan's Seiko. East Asia appeared to be "re-colonized" by Japanese corporations. The world clamored to learn Japanese. All around the world, Japan Inc. was on the offensive.

Think back to 1980s pop culture. Remember the sequel to *Back to the Future* in which Michael J. Fox gets to see a glimpse of his future? His boss was Japanese and was calling him on a video conference phone from Tokyo—reflecting the widespread belief at the time that we would *all* have Japanese bosses in just a few short years.

The Japanese stock market played its part in the affair (Figure 3.1). Share prices shot through the roof in the 1980s, and by the middle of the decade, they were in a speculative bubble. Between 1985 and 1990 the Nikkei tripled, hitting a high just shy of 40,000 in December of 1989.

Not to be outdone, the Japanese real estate bubble dwarfed that of the stock market (Figure 3.2). Home prices in Tokyo far outpaced incomes, making 100-year multigenerational mortgages a necessity. At its peak, Japanese property was worth four times that of the entire United States, and the area around the Imperial Palace alone was gauged to be more valuable than the state of California, Silicon Valley and all.

Those bubble days are long gone, and today we see a very different Japan. Japanese stocks and urban land are still down 75% and 70% respectively from their peak nearly two decades ago. Japan has spent the last twenty years in and out of recession, unable to gain any real momentum. So what caused Japan to fall into this long, dark economic hibernation?

## Figure 3.1 Japan Nikkei Stock Index

Japanese stocks are still down 75% from their all-time highs reached during the bubble.

Source: Bloomberg

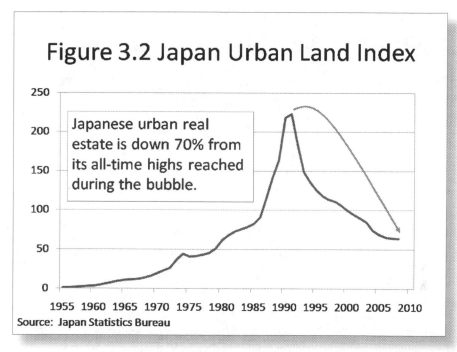

Figure 3.2 Japan Urban Land Index

Japanese urban real estate is down 70% from its all-time highs reached during the bubble.

Source: Japan Statistics Bureau

As you might guess, it was largely the falling desire of Japanese consumers. Low consumer demand due to the aging of the population meant low profits for Japanese companies, which in turn led to decreased hiring and even lower demand. A vicious cycle developed with no way out.

This phenomenon could have been easily predicted, however, if you simply knew where to look. Essentially, what the Japanese were going through was the natural demographic cycle of an aging country that spends less and saves more. The situation was exacerbated by an over-leveraged, over-indebted population.

Does this sound familiar? This scenario—lower demand, lower profits, lower production, lower demand—is clearly already playing out in the United States as well.

But surely nothing like that could happen in the United States, many pundits insist. Fed Chairman Ben Bernanke has effectively lowered the Federal Funds target rate to zero. The Bush and Obama administrations launched the biggest fiscal stimulus drive in history. Would this not save us from falling into a deflationary trap like Japan? Unfortunately, the historical precedent suggests it will not.

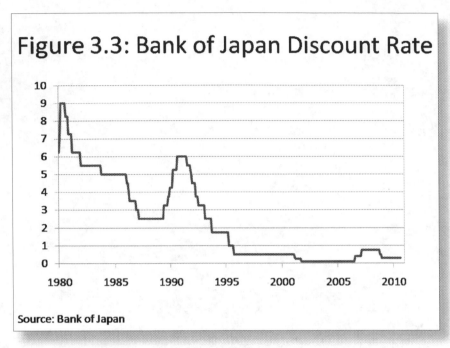

**Figure 3.3: Bank of Japan Discount Rate**

Source: Bank of Japan

As the Japanese crisis wore on, the Bank of Japan cut interest rates from 6% to zero (Figure 3.3), essentially giving money away in the hopes that someone would spend it. In the standard monetarist formula, lowering interest rates spurs both consumption and investment. As the reward for saving money gets smaller, the incentive to spend it or invest it gets bigger. But a curious thing happened on the way to the fish market; interest rates dropped, but savings remained high. Consumer spending stayed flat and then fell. New investment in productive assets stalled; Japanese businesses already had more than enough capacity. In the 1930s, John Maynard Keynes likened this kind of situation to "pushing on a string." It could also be compared to herding cats. Injecting liquidity into the system and making money available to lend is useless if no one is interested in borrowing.

That did not stop Japan from trying, of course. The Bank of Japan aggressively monetized the county's debts, causing the monetary base to soar (Figure 3.4). As I suggested in the previous chapter, when the monetary base expands rapidly the result is generally inflation or even hyperinflation. The German Weimar Republic of the 1920s comes to mind, which led to a little man with an odd little mustache who brought the entire world to the brink of ruin in World War II. But the Japanese economy resisted this convention. Even while the monetary base expanded, the money supply fell from over 12% to less than 0. "Plunged" (Figure 3.5) might be a better word. Sound familiar?

Figure 3.4: Japan Monetary Base

Japan's central bank "printed" money to stimulate the economy.

Source: Bank of Japan

Figure 3.5: Japan Money Supply % Change from Previous Year

Source: Bank of Japan

The Bank of Japan made credit available. But with the value of their loans having fallen significantly below the market price of the underlying collateral, Japanese banks were not interested in lending. They became "zombies," technically insolvent yet continuing to roll over existing loans, all the while absorbing loanable funds that might have been better put to use elsewhere.

Japan did not stop with central bank monetary policy, of course. The government launched countless expensive fiscal stimulus programs, most of which produced barely a ripple. Much like the Roosevelt Administration during the Depression, the Japanese used massive government deficit spending to spur demand, but the Japanese did this on an even bigger scale. The once fiscally conservative Japanese government went on the largest public works spending spree in history, boosting its budget deficits and government debts to levels rarely seen in developed countries (Figure 3.6).

Today, Japan has 30 times the amount of land covered in concrete as the United States, adjusting for the size difference in the two countries, and over 2,800 river dams[3], but the Japanese version of the Tennessee Valley Authority could not possibly hope to spend enough money to compensate for a lack of private consumer spending.

Take another look at Figure 3.6. Japan's government debt is now 200% of the country's annual GDP. This is unprecedented for an industrialized country, and it will be a major impediment for a very long time. I'll return to this theme in a later chapter, offering insight from Harvard professor Kenneth Rogoff and University of Maryland professor Carmen Reinhart. But for now, let us continue our discussion of inflation.

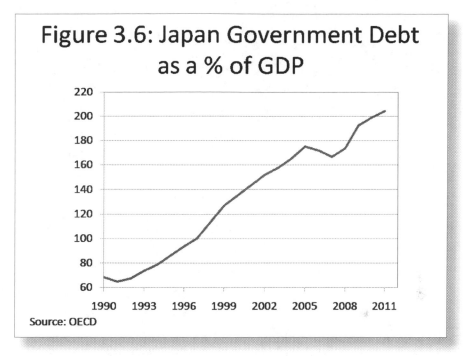

# Figure 3.6: Japan Government Debt as a % of GDP

Source: OECD

One might think that Japan's government spending binge would have stimulated demand and ignited the desired inflation. Nothing could be further from the truth.

For any readers who continue to believe that the U.S. government's actions will lead to inflation (and are busily selling stocks to buy gold), take a long look at Figures 3.7 and 3.8. The Japanese government *wanted* inflation, and couldn't make it happen. As you can see in Figure 3.7, Japan started to have severe disinflation in late 1990, which fell into full-blown deflation by 1995. Japan has struggled to rise out of deflation ever since.

Figure 3.8 is an index of Japan's price level. Prices in Japan haven't risen in 18 years. *The last time Japan had sustained inflation, Bill Clinton was still the governor of Arkansas!*

Figure 3.7: Japan Inflation
CPI Year-Over-Year % Change

Source: Bloomberg

Figure 3.8: Japan Inflation
Consumer Price Index

Prices in Japan haven't risen in over 18 years

Source: Bloomberg

Of course, the United States is not Japan. This is a different country in a different decade with a host of unique issues. But returning to the Mark Twain quote, history does rhyme. If I have inundated you with charts in the last two chapters, it is to drive home this important point. Our situation today is similar to that of Japan two decades ago, but not the *same*.

In both countries there was a debt-fueled bubble in property that was followed by a colossal bust and a prolonged period of economic stagnation. I believe that the situation here is grave, but I want to stress that I do not believe that it is quite as bad as Japan. Even more importantly, I want to make it clear that there are ways to make money in this market that do not involve a great degree of risk. The 1930s was arguably the worst decade for stocks this country has ever seen, yet during that period the most millionaires in American history were created. And there were stretches of multiple years in the 1930s when the stock market actually did quite well.

Eighteen years from now, I do not expect us to still be suffering from deflation. We will have our problems, of course. The funding issues of Social Security and Medicare and the ballooning federal debt are not going away any time soon. But Japan has issues that we simply do not have.

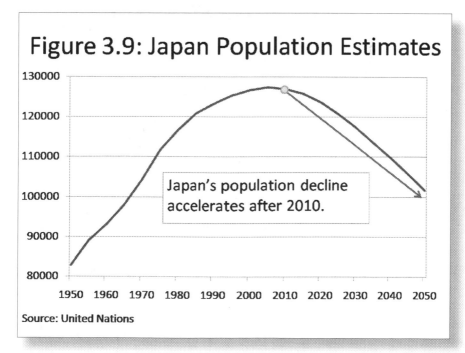

# Figure 3.9: Japan Population Estimates

Japan's population decline accelerates after 2010.

**Source: United Nations**

Japan's population is aging rapidly and is actually shrinking as deaths exceed births (Figure 3.9). Imagine the difficulty of running a retail-oriented business in Japan or even a restaurant. Every year, the base of potential customers gets smaller, and those that are left are older and less likely to buy anything. This is a slow-motion train wreck happening before our very eyes.

Japan will almost certainly collapse in one way or another. The government has run debts that it can never hope to repay, and the citizenry is slowing dying of old age. Currently their debt is in excess of 200% of GDP. This has forced S&P to cut Japan's credit rating to AA-, four marks below the best AAA rating. The only way out of the pending debt crisis is to devalue the debt through inflation. The problem with this is that inflation hurts the elderly far worse than anyone else due to their reliance on savings and pension payments, and Japan has the highest percentage of elderly citizens of any country in the world—elderly people who vote and who would no doubt punish any politician who wrecked their retirement dreams. As I have made painstakingly clear, Japan has also attempted to generate inflation for twenty years now and has failed.

I do understand that there are many who believe that the United States is also heading for hyperinflation. However, Japan is almost twenty years into its crisis, and as much as it is trying to create inflation, it hasn't happened yet. It is entirely possible that the United States will succumb to an inflationary spiral at some point. But if Japan is our guide, it will not happen any time soon.

"This time is different," is a common reply I hear when I use historical examples. But is it really?

The next chapter is dedicated to debunking a certain kind of denial I call the "this time is different" syndrome. If you are making the correct comparisons, events today are not at all different from those in the past.

The good news is that by virtue of being here today, we humans have proven that we persevere. Crises are not fun, but we do survive them and life goes on. The bad news is that history suggests we have a rough road in front of us.

# Chapter 4:

# This Time is Different

King Solomon had it all figured out when, more than 3,000 years ago, he wrote, *"There is nothing new under the sun."*4 He was a tired old man who had seen it all and had the good sense and humility to realize that his circumstance wasn't all that unique. You can imagine him staring out of his palace and asking himself, "Is there anything of which one can say, 'Look! This is something new? It was here already, long ago; it was here before our time.'"

It's a shame so few have heeded his observation; otherwise we might have avoided the housing bubble and meltdown of the 2000s—and every other financial crisis in human history.

In their recent book, *This Time Is Different5*, Carmen Reinhart and Kenneth Rogoff draw the same conclusion as old Solomon. This time it's *not* different. It never is, and it probably never will be. As they state in the introduction, "Our basic message is simple: We have been here before. No matter how different the latest financial frenzy or crisis always appears, there are usually remarkable similarities with past experience from other countries and from history." The names, faces and financial instruments might change, but the plot does not. And neither does the ending.

I am a big believer in the repetitiveness of history. There are generational cycles, as Strauss and Howe have outlined in their work.6 There is the boom and bust cycle of the economy, as explained by various economists, including John Maynard Keynes (who coined the phrase "animal spirits"), Friedrich von Hayek, and Joseph Schumpeter.

There are cycles in stock and commodities markets as well.

The persistent occurrence of boom and bust cycles has been noted in Charles Kindleberger's book *Manias, Panics, and Crashes: A History of Financial Crises*, and in Charles Mackay's classic *Extraordinary Popular Delusions and the Madness of Crowds*, among others. What separates Reinhart and Rogoff's efforts from those of their predecessors is the sophistication of the delivery. Kindleberger and Mackay take a narrative approach, telling the story of each financial mania like a play-by-play announcer and noting similarities among them. Reinhart and Rogoff instead take a quantitative approach, building their analysis from a massive database that "encompasses the entire world and goes back as far as twelfth-century China."

From this database they can tell that that, on average, ***government debt rises by 86 percent during the three years following a banking crisis***. So, while the Obama Administration's record deficits may be unsettling, they are certainly nothing new in history. Reinhart and Rogoff point out that the increase in government debt is a much better gauge of the severity of a crisis than the explicit cost of bailouts alone. The increase in government debt reflects both explicit costs and the damage done to the real economy, seen in lower tax receipts. We are seeing this today at all levels of government—from Washington, DC, to local neighborhood homeowners' associations.

In this chapter, we're going to take a look at some of Reinhart and Rogoff's findings in an attempt to keep the current crisis in perspective. Their book has *far* too much information for us to cover in one short chapter, but I'll attempt to glean the most important parts for our purposes.

It Starts With Debt

In previous chapters I have focused heavily on the role of debt in the recent crisis and on the ongoing, multi-decade crisis in Japan. Reinhart and Rogoff would appear to agree:

> If there is one common theme to the vast range of crises we consider in this book, it is that excessive debt accumulation, whether it be by the government, banks, corporations, or consumers, often poses greater systemic risks than it seems during a boom....

Such large-scale debt buildups pose risks because they make an economy vulnerable to crises of confidence, particularly when debt is short term and needs to be constantly refinanced. Debt-fueled booms all too often provide false affirmation of a government's policies, a financial institution's ability to make outsized profits, or a country's standard of living. Most of these booms end badly. Of course, debt instruments are crucial to all economies, ancient and modern, but balancing the risk and opportunities of debt is always a challenge, a challenge policy makers, investors, and ordinary citizens must never forget.

To illustrate how debt makes crises significantly more serious, the authors consider the case of the tech bubble and bust in 2001. While the amount of wealth destruction in the market crash was enormous and had a real effect on the retirement plans of millions of Americans, the overall damage to the economy was minor. We had a run-of-the-mill recession in 2001, which was worsened by the September 11 terror attacks. But not even the destruction of the Twin Towers, in the heart of America's financial center, could rival the damage done to the economy by the mortgage debt crisis that hit just six years later.

As Reinhart and Rogoff write, "What is certainly clear is that again and again, countries, banks, individuals, and firms take on excessive debt in good times without enough awareness of the risks that will follow when the inevitable recession hits."

Here, the authors echo Hyman Minsky, whose work has enjoyed a comeback in recent years. Minsky's pet theory was the Financial Instability Hypothesis.[7] Minsky believed that financial stability led to its own demise. During healthy economic times, borrowers and lenders alike let their guard down, lured by rising asset prices and a lack of volatility. As banks lend more and more to eager borrowers, asset prices rise, often to inflated bubble levels. Eventually, the debt-fueled bubble becomes unsustainable, and the whole thing collapses like a house of cards. Only afterward do lenders and borrowers regain the conservatism that originally allowed for stability—and the cycle continues.

Sound familiar? Lending standards for a new mortgage are stiff today, *after* the crisis. It's like a never-ending cycle of closing the barn door after the horse has already bolted.

On Black Swans

Nassim Nicholas Taleb's pet phrase, "black swan," is well known in financial circles, although most people have only a murky idea as to what it means. A black swan is a high-impact, low probability event. It's something that you would never expect to happen, so when it *does* happen, it's a big deal.

However, as Taleb points out repeatedly in his work, black swans are not all that uncommon. In fact, they are an all too common occurrence in financial markets.

Reinhart and Rogoff, although they never use the phrase "black swan," arrive at the same end. They conclude that "rare" events are often not all that rare when viewed in a longer historical context.

Reinhart and Rogoff write,

> Above all, our emphasis is on looking at long spans of history to catch sight of "rare" events that are all too often forgotten, although they turn out to be far more common and similar than people seem to think….

> An event that was rare in that twenty-five-year span may not be all that rare when placed in a longer historical context. After all, a researcher stands only a one-in-four chance of observing a "hundred-year flood" in twenty-five years' worth of data.

Ironically, the historical crisis that most resembles our current one is the 1907 panic—which hit pretty close to exactly one hundred years before the 2008 meltdown.

Financial Crises By the Numbers

In their cross-sectional study, Reinhart and Rogoff dissect the anatomy of a financial crisis and find three common characteristics:

1. Asset market collapses are deep and prolonged. ***Declines in real housing prices average 35% stretched out over six years, whereas stock bear market declines average 56% over three and a half years.***

Interestingly, the current crisis is atypical in that the housing and stock market declines came much faster and harder than the average. Of course, the bubble in housing prices preceding the crisis was more than three times larger than average, implying that this one is likely to have further to go. As Reinhart and Rogoff point out, Japan is also a notable exception to the averages. Japan's housing and stock market declines have been virtually uninterrupted for *two decades*.

2.  The aftermath of a banking crisis generally will include large declines in output and employment. The unemployment rate rises an average of seven percentage points during the downward phase of the cycle, which lasts on average more than four years. Output (GDP) falls more than nine percent on average over roughly two years. This shows that, in general, employment is a lagging indicator.

    The U.S. is pretty close to the mark in unemployment, up roughly 6% to just shy of 10%. GDP decline has been nowhere near the 9% average, at least not yet. Let us hope it doesn't get there.

3.  Finally, as mentioned earlier, government debts explode during a financial crisis, rising an average of 86% in real terms in the major post–World War II episodes. Currently, gross U.S. federal debt is up roughly 40%. This number implies that the U.S. government still has quite a bit of deficit spending to do.

Remember, these numbers are averages, which implies that roughly half of the crises in recorded history were more severe than these numbers would suggest. The sheer size of the American housing boom indicates that the bust we are now in could have some staying power.

But isn't the economy recovering? Of course it is. However, it's recovering from very low levels, and demand remains far below the pre-crisis highs. Demographic trends also suggest a rocky road ahead.

It is my view that the current bust will be significantly longer and more severe than the averages listed above but that it will probably not be as bad as the Japanese crisis by at least some measures. Let us hope I am not wrong about that.

## Growth in a Time of Debt

After the publication of Reinhart and Rogoff's *This Time Is Different*, the authors did a 2010 follow-up white paper titled "Growth in a Time of Debt."[8]

With all of the talk of "double dip" recession in the news, Reinhart and Rogoff's paper is a timely analysis. We will find out soon enough whether the United States has technically entered recession again or if we narrowly avoid it with a period of very slow growth. It's my view that the entire discussion is an exercise in futility, comparable to the debate among medieval Catholic theologians who argued *passionately* about how many angels could balance on the head of a pin.

Whether reported GDP contracts or expands modestly, the basic fundamentals have not changed. We still have a financial system dominated by large banks with impaired balance sheets that are unable or unwilling to lend. We still have a housing sector that would appear *highly* susceptible to further declines given the never-ending supply of new foreclosures. And we still have the largest generation in history—the Baby Boomers—who need desperately to downsize their lives and save for retirement.

When GDP numbers are released, they tell us what happened *last* quarter. How, exactly, is this useful information?

Of particular concern these days is the rate of growth in the national debt. As a result of the bailouts and the collapse in tax receipts, **the Federal debt has ballooned to $13.2 trillion**, $8.7 trillion of which is held by the public. There is genuine worry that this expansion of debt will lead to financial instability and will have long-term effects on economic growth. As I mentioned earlier, in *This Time is Different*, Reinhart and Rogoff found that central government debt rises on average by about 86% within three years after the crisis. If the historical pattern holds, we still have a ways to go.

Unlike most economic historians, who take a narrative approach to compare past crises to the present, Reinhart and Rogoff use a quantitative approach. There is no "fluff" in their analysis; it is based on cold, hard statistics.

The two academics compiled a new database covering forty-four countries and spanning about hundred years. The dataset incorporates over 3,700 annual observations and, per Reinhart and Rogoff, "covers a wide range of political systems, institutions, exchange rate arrangements, and historic circumstances."

In exploring the relationship between government debt and economic growth the authors made some interesting observations.

1. The relationship between government debt and real GDP growth is weak for debt/GDP ratios below a threshold of 90 percent of GDP. **Above 90 percent, median growth rates fall by one percent, and average growth falls considerably more.** We find that the threshold for public debt is similar in advanced and emerging economies.

2. **Emerging markets face lower thresholds** for external debt (public and private)—which is usually denominated in a foreign currency. When external debt reaches 60 percent of GDP, annual growth declines by about two percent; for higher levels, growth rates are roughly cut in half.

3. **There is no apparent link between inflation and public debt levels for the advanced countries as a group.** The story is entirely different for emerging markets, where inflation rises sharply as debt increases.

**Figure 4.1** illustrates the increase in public debt among major economies since 2007. For the five countries with housing/mortgage related financial crises (Iceland, Ireland, Spain, the United Kingdom, and the United States), average debt levels are up by about 75 percent, well on track to reach or surpass the Reinhart and Rogoff's three-year 86 percent benchmark. Perhaps most interesting is that the United States—where the entire mess started—has seen the least accumulation of debt of the group. Americans have justifiably begun to grow weary of bailouts and deficit spending, but compared to Iceland, Ireland, the UK, Spain, Norway, and Australia, the United States' recent bout of fiscal hemorrhaging would almost appear mild!

Looking at total debt as a percentage of GDP, however, the United

States looks a little worse. By Reinhart and Rogoff's estimates, US debt/GDP stands at 84 percent—dangerously close to the 90 percent threshold at which debt begins to crimp growth. Recent releases indicate that the United States has actually already breached 90 percent.

This is still barely half of Japan's 182 percent—a number so high that Japan cannot hope to meaningfully lower it for a long time. But at 90 percent, it is certainly time for Americans to start worrying. Expect GDP growth to be muted going forward.

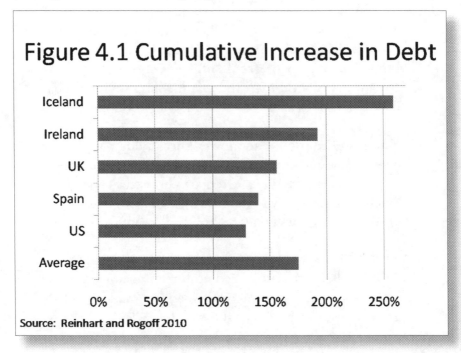

It is easy enough to understand why debt starts to crimp growth once it gets sufficiently high. Eventually, in order to appease lenders, taxes have to rise or spending has to slow. Both are contractionary to the economy.

The other solution—and one that has many Americans and Europeans nervously buying gold to hedge—**is that governments will intentionally ignite inflation as a way to make existing debts shrink in real terms**. This makes intuitive sense, and indeed it would appear that Ben Bernanke was attempting to do exactly that when he doubled the monetary base in 2008 and early 2009. But as I explained at length in prior chapters, deflation, not inflation, is a more likely scenario. The continued deleveraging of the private sector, prolonged by the Baby Boomers passing their peak spending years, will negate the inflationary policies of the Fed.

Reinhart and Rogoff's data would appear to support my view. Figure 4.2, which is somewhat hard to interpret at first glance, compares GDP growth (bars) and inflation (line) by various debt "buckets." The median inflation rate, at 4%, is considerably lower for high-debt countries (those with debt/GDP of over 90%) vs. low-debt countries (those with debt/GDP of less than 30%). Using the average instead of the median, we actually have mild deflation for a high-debt country. This is certainly the case in Japan today.

## Figure 4.2 GDP Growth With Debt

Source: Reinhart and Rogoff 2010

One question begs to be asked: Why is 90 percent the threshold?

Why does growth stall at 90 percent and not, say, 50 percent or 180 percent? Rogoff and Reinhart have no definitive answers to this question. Their data tells them what is; it does not tell them why.

We can, however, draw one, big meaningful conclusion from all of this. A rigorous empirical analysis of past financial crises would support my view that the coming years will be marked by slow economic growth and the persistent threat of deflation. That is, unless "this time is different."

## Complexity and Collapse

On a related note, I want to mention an interesting article published by Niall Ferguson, the author of *The Ascent of Money*. Ferguson published an article in *Foreign Affairs* titled "Complexity and Collapse"[9] that ties in nicely with Reinhart and Rogoff's work. Ferguson's focus is on "imperial overstretch," and that is a topic outside of the scope of this book, but the article's insights on debt are instructive. Ferguson writes,

> There is no better illustration of the life cycle of a great power than *The Course of Empire*, a series of five paintings by Thomas Cole that hang in the New York Historical Society... In *The Course of Empire*, he beautifully captured a theory of imperial rise and fall to which most people remain in thrall to this day.
>
> Each of the five imagined scenes depicts the mouth of a great river beneath a rocky outcrop. In the first, *The Savage State*, a lush wilderness is populated by a handful of hunter-gatherers eking out a primitive existence at the break of a stormy dawn. The second picture, *The Arcadian or Pastoral State*, is of an agrarian idyll: the inhabitants have cleared the trees, planted fields, and built an elegant Greek temple. The third and largest of the paintings is *The Consummation of Empire*. Now, the landscape is covered by a magnificent marble entrepôt, and the contented farmer-philosophers of the previous tableau have been replaced by a throng of opulently clad merchants, proconsuls, and citizen-consumers. It is midday in the life cycle. Then comes *Destruction*. The city is ablaze, its citizens fleeing an invading horde that rapes and pillages beneath a brooding evening sky. Finally, the moon rises over the fifth painting, *Desolation*. There is not a living soul to be seen, only a few decaying columns and colonnades overgrown by briars and ivy.

Popular sentiment would suggest we are somewhere in the late stages of "Consummation of Empire" or early stages of "Destruction." In any event, the view is that we are in for a long, protracted downfall as debt and bad demographics create roadblocks to a sustainable recovery.

Ferguson would argue that this is a fundamentally flawed way to look at history. History does *not* follow long cycles of rise and fall. Instead it is "arrhythmic—at times almost stationary, but also capable of accelerating suddenly, like a sports car." Collapse does not happen over time but comes suddenly, "like a thief in the night."

Ferguson suggests that great powers and empires (and I would suggest modern industrial economies) are complex systems that operate somewhere between order and disorder, "on the edge of chaos." Such systems—like Japan's economy, for example—can appear to be stable even while they are quietly and constantly deteriorating behind the scenes.

At some point, however, complex systems reach a "tipping point," to use a term coined by Malcolm Gladwell. A very small trigger—the proverbial straw that breaks the camel's back—can set off a "phase transition from a benign equilibrium to a crisis."

Ferguson uses several examples from history to show that societies do not typically follow a slow decline. The destruction of Rome, an empire that lasted for centuries, happened in just a few short decades. The Ottoman and Hapsburg Empires too collapsed almost overnight. As more recent examples, Ferguson uses the British Empire and the Soviet Union. In retrospect, it seems obvious that Britain's global empire was unsustainable. After all, one of the rallying cries of the American Revolution was that an island had no authority to rule a continent. Yet was the impending collapse of the British Empire obvious to anyone in the decades before it happened? Britain was on the winning side of both world wars, but less than a decade after the end of World War II, she had lost substantially her entire empire. Similarly, it is easy for us today to argue that communism was doomed to fail in the Soviet Union. But ask the Baby Boomers if it was obvious to them.

I had the good fortune to visit the Soviet Union in 1984 when I was attending University of London. It wasn't easy for an American to travel there then, but I joined up with a group of British students. It was clear that their market was absolutely primitive in comparison to ours. There were barely any cars on the road, with most belonging to party officials. The technology was archaic, and a copy of Playboy magazine or just a few western cigarettes were valuable currency. Regardless, there were still no signs of obvious fracture. It wasn't pretty, but it appeared solid and stable. Nobody could have guessed that within just a few short years, the "Evil Empire" would collapse with breathtaking speed.

As Ferguson points out, historians love to tell history as narrative story, but in doing so they minimize the complexity of the real world. They make outcomes appear obvious in retrospect when at the time they were not obvious at all. This is what Nassim Taleb called "the narrative fallacy" in *The Black Swan*. *Post hoc, ergo propter hoc.* "After this, therefore because of this," or in other words, "if it happened this way, it *had* to happen this way."

I want to make something clear: I am not a "doom and gloomer" who forecasts the fall of America. Not at all. I believe that we have difficult years ahead of us, but collapse—if it happens—is not something that I foresee happening in this lifetime. We might scale back our foreign policy ambitions—or we might not. But economic collapse strikes me as unlikely.

I'm not so sure about Japan, however. Using Ferguson's terms, Japan is in a state of stable equilibrium. The country's demographics are crumbling and government debt continues to expand at an alarming rate. But life is going on as usual for most Japanese. The financial system is still functioning. In fact, Japanese bond yields are still near record lows, and the yen remains a relatively strong currency.

But how long can this continue? According to Reinhart and Rogoff, debt begins to significantly crimp economic growth once it hits 90% of GDP. Japan is currently at 200%, and growth has certainly stalled.

It remains to be seen what the endgame for Japan will be. But if Ferguson's analysis holds, Japan's collapse, if or when it happens, will be much quicker and more abrupt that anyone expects. Holders of Japanese yen should keep that in mind.

# Chapter 5:
# The Granddaddy of All Debt Bubbles

If you think that Fed Chairman Ben Bernanke is unpopular, consider the tragic case of Takahashi Korekiyo, who served as Bank of Japan governor from 1911-1913 and as finance minister and prime minister in the 1920s and 1930s.

Mr. Takahashi helped to pull Japan out of the Great Depression with aggressive monetary stimulus (or "quantitative easing," in the popular jargon of today) and deficit spending. Unfortunately, like a man who joins the mafia, he found that he couldn't get out. The Japanese economy had become dependent on stimulus, and when Mr. Takahashi finally decided to risk it by tightening monetary policy and cutting government spending, he was assassinated by a group of rogue army officers.

Ben Bernanke is at little risk of meeting such a fate, though there are certainly plenty in Congress who would love to see him kicked out of the job. If certain members of the Tea Party had their way, the Chairman might meet the fate of John Law, the Scottish adventurer who, as France's first central banker, became the most powerful man in international finance—and the wealthiest man in the world—before having to flee penniless into exile and obscurity.

In the last chapter, we took a look at historical financial crises and made general comments about what happens during the bubble and the bust that follows. In this chapter, I want to recount the unfortunate story of the first major debt-fueled bubble and bust in Western history—the **Mississippi Land Scheme.**

John Law presided over the Mississippi Land Scheme, which was abetted by the creation of the first modern central bank in Europe, the French Banque Generale (later re-christened the Banque Royale). Law was an interesting character—a gentleman gambler with a taste for wealth, wine, women and power. His financial career began in the gaming halls of Europe after escaping a death sentence in England for killing a man in 1694, allegedly over the affections of a woman.

One might ask, how did this murdering degenerate come to control the financial destiny of France, then the most powerful nation in Europe? It was a long, circuitous path.

John Law was born in 1671 to an Edinburgh goldsmith. Goldsmiths were the foundation of the early European banking system, performing basic deposit and lending functions; they would take deposits of gold coin and issue paper certificates which could be redeemed at any time for the gold they represented.

Learning the basic tricks of the trade from his father—and having a gift for calculating odds that made him dangerous in Europe's casinos—Law was exceptionally well positioned for a career in finance.

Law spent nine years on the run in Continental Europe after escaping England and amassed a small fortune before returning to Scotland. (English warrants were not honored in Scotland at the time.) The Scotland that Law returned to was in the midst of a crisis after a disastrous colonial venture in Panama that wiped out the savings of much of the country's citizenry. Law's proposal to get the Scottish economy moving again—which was defeated by the Scottish parliament—was the issuance of paper money backed by the land owned by the government.

You see, monetary conditions in the wake of the crisis were extraordinarily tight. Given that there was a shortage of physical gold (as most of it was lost in the Panama debacle) banks and private citizens alike were hoarding what little cash they did have. The money supply was diminished and the *velocity* of money was in free fall. (Sound familiar? A collapse in the velocity of money is a common occurrence in nearly all post-bubble crises, and the American housing and debt crisis of 2008 was no exception.)

Law believed that paper money was preferable to gold or silver coinage for several reasons. Paper money is highly portable and interchangeable, making it more convenient than gold or silver as a medium of exchange and facilitator of economic activity. Law was correct in this observation and noted—as Adam Smith would write more than 70 years later in *The Wealth of Nations*—that a country's wealth should be measured by its output, not by its holdings of precious metals.

Unfortunately, paper money can also be printed at will. More on that later.

Though rejected in his native Scotland, Law's ideas would soon find fertile ground on the other side of the English Channel. Upon his death, Louis XIV—the "Sun King"—had left France virtually bankrupt. As it turned out, building Versailles and spending decades at war cost money—a *lot* of money. About three billion livres, while annual tax revenues were a mere 145 million livres. To put this in perspective, the official U.S. Treasury debt held by the public is $9.1 trillion, and annual tax revenues are $2.2 trillion. That makes the U.S. debt-to-income ratio 4 times, while the ratio that Louis XIV bequeathed to his son was an almost unfathomable *21 times!*

The interest payments on the debt took up 120 million of the 145 livres in revenues—leaving a mere 25 million to finance the rest of the French government's expenses. Given that annual expenses were 142 million livres, the French crown depended on further access to credit to keep afloat. Suffice it to say that France was a bad credit risk.

Then along came a certain Scotsman.

Because Louis XV was only a young boy when his father died, his uncle Philippe II, the Duc d'Orleans, became the Regent of France. Philippe was in a bind and was willing to try something—anything—to avoid default and collapse. And John Law appeared to have the answer— the creation of new money by a powerful government-chartered bank that would be used to pay off the existing debts. Law would issue stock in the new bank and would use the proceeds of the IPO to buy back government debt. He would also take deposits in coin but issue loans and withdrawals in paper. How is *that* for quantitative easing?

As Bill Bonner and Addison Wiggin put it in their telling of the story,

> On May 5, 1716, the Banque Generale was founded with 6 million livres in capital and was assured success from the beginning. The Duc declared all taxes must henceforth be paid with notes issued by Law's bank [making Law's notes legal tender]...

> The French national debt at the time would, today, have
> already been seriously downgraded by Moody's. The billets
> d'etat—government bonds issued under Louis XIV to pay for
> his extravagance—were essentially junk bonds…
>
> The challenge for Law was to buy back the outstanding
> government debt at the market rate of 21.50 without driving up
> the price. If investors discovered the government was reclaiming
> their billets d'etat and that Philippe II could effectively save the
> royal finances, they would certainly begin asking more than
> 21.50 per billet. Law solved the problem by offering the bank
> shares exclusively in exchange for the government bonds.

This initial move only retired a small fraction of the national debt,
but Law was far from finished.

Law built trust in his new paper money by making it redeemable for
the full par value in gold coin and went so far as to say that any banker
unable to meet redemptions on demand "deserved death." His rhetoric
worked. The French bought into the scheme hook, line, and sinker.

In a truly unusual sign of the times, Law's paper currency actually
traded at a 15% *premium* to comparable gold coins one year into the
scheme. As Law anticipated, the jolt in both the money supply and the
velocity of money jump-started the French economy.

France might have prospered had Law stopped there, gradually
paying off its debts through a mixture of economic growth and mild
inflation, but alas he got cocky. To pay off the country's remaining
debts in one grand swoop, Law launched the next phase of his scheme.
As Bonner and Wiggin continue,

> Law convinced Philippe II to back a trading company with
> monopoly trading rights over the Mississippi River and France's
> land claim in Louisiana. Shares in the new company would be
> offered to the public, and investors would only be allowed to
> buy them with the remaining billets d'etat on the market [i.e.,
> the existing French Crown junk bonds]. So begins the famed
> Mississippi Scheme.

Law's new venture, which would come to be known as the Compagnie des Indes, was granted all the possessions of its competitors—the Senegal Company, the China Company, and the French East India company—giving it exclusive French trading rights for the Mississippi River, Louisiana, China, East India, and South America. Law's enterprise also received the sole right to mint royal coins for nine years; it was allowed to act as the royal tax collector for the same amount of time; and it was granted a monopoly on all tobacco trade under French rule...

Immediately after the initial public offering (IPO), applications for shares in the Compagnie des Indes started coming in from all levels of society. So many, in fact, that it took the staff at the bank weeks to sort through all the applications. Traders, merchants, dukes, counts, and marquises crowded into the little rue Quincampoix and waited for hours to find out if their subscriptions had been granted. When the final list of subscribers was announced, Law and his awaiting public learned that the shares had been oversubscribed by a factor of six. The immediate result? Shares in the Compagnie des Indes skyrocketed in value.[10]

The Compagnie des Indes—popularly called the Mississippi Company—was France's answer to the Dutch East India Company, but with one critical difference: the Dutch company actually had profitable trading routes. The French trading company had the mosquito-infested bog we today call Louisiana and little else.

The investors that piled in were buying shares in a company without any real business model. How exactly Law intended to make money in Louisiana—a land of tepid swamps, not mountains of gold—was never fully explained. Though we can shake our heads at the silly Frenchmen in retrospect, it is easy to understand their enthusiasm. They were trading in rather junky junk bonds for an exciting opportunity in the New World—an investment that, while ridiculous in retrospect, was no more absurd than buying tech stocks in 1999 or Miami condos in 2005. The "animal spirits" that characterize all financial bubbles were fueled by an exceptionally loose monetary policy, with predictable results.

Impressed with the success of the original paper banknotes, Philippe II decided to expand Law's operation. He renamed the Banque Generale the Banque Royale, made it an official organ of the Crown, and proceeded to expand the money supply by 16 times its previous amount, later increasing it by even more. Suddenly, Ben Bernanke's much maligned "QE2" would seem tame by comparison!

Much of the new money went directly into shares of the Mississippi Company. In a matter of months, the share price rose from 500 livres to 10,000 livres (see Figure 5.1), creating a new class of *nouveau riche* dubbed "millionaires." A cycle developed whereby demand for the Mississippi shares would create demand for new paper currency with which to buy them. And Philippe and Law were only too happy to oblige.

**Law's central bank allowed investors to borrow money at low interest rates using their Mississippi shares as collateral**. This would be like the Federal Reserve lending you money directly to buy shares of a new, unproven technology start-up company using your existing shares of the company as collateral. This set up something of a self-contained Ponzi scheme. (The excesses in the mortgage markets during the mid-2000s, in which government-sponsored entities provided almost unlimited capital for additional mortgage loans on increasingly generous terms shows that, as the French say, "Plus ça change, plus c'est la même chose." The more things change, the more they stay the same.)

In the later stages of the scheme, the Banque and Mississippi Company were effectively merged and there was no discernable difference between bank notes, Mississippi shares, and the old government debt. The system evolved from a paper system backed by a gold standard to paper system backed by Mississippi shares which were in turn "backed" by land in Louisiana. (How the currency would be redeemed for land was, again, never really explained.)

**Figure 5.1: Mississippi Company Share Price**

Source: Francois Velde

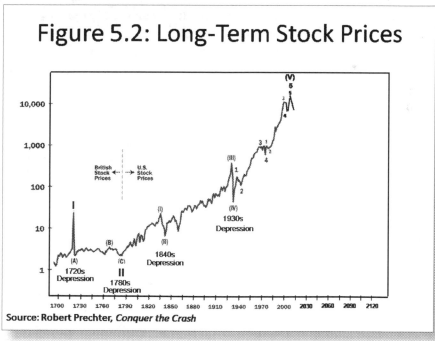

**Figure 5.2: Long-Term Stock Prices**

Source: Robert Prechter, *Conquer the Crash*

The entire scheme began to unravel when Law attempted to gently deflate the bubble, which had already led to hyperinflation throughout the French economy and which had spread to neighboring England as well. The surge in liquidity created by Law's scheme spilled across the English Channel and helped to inflate the South Sea Bubble, which had its own excesses nearly as legendary as those of France.

When investors attempted to redeem their banknotes for gold, it quickly became obvious that there was not enough metal coinage to back the banknotes in circulation. The bank stopped payment on its notes, and Law was forced to flee the country in disgrace. Shares in the Mississippi Company fell all the way back to their issue price, destroying both the newly rich and the established order alike.

The only thing more painful than hyperinflation is the inevitable deflation that follows. When the credit markets seized up, the supply and velocity of money plummeted as desperate Frenchmen scurried to dump their worthless banknotes and shares. France and her middle and upper classes were ruined, and the monarchy was discredited—setting the stage for the bloody French Revolution a generation later. The French developed a strong distaste for banking and capital markets that arguably lingers to this day. The debacle set back the development of modern capitalism in France by decades.

As for the investors, they endured a bear market that would make modern investors shudder. Take a look at Figure 5.2. Though reliable French stock market data is hard to come by, we can use British data as a proxy. As I mentioned before, London had a market bubble of its own—the South Sea Bubble—that coincided with the Mississippi Bubble. This is the sharp spike you see around the year 1720.

What followed was *70 years* of bear market conditions. Stocks did not meaningfully rise again until the 1790s. So much for "stocks for the long run" or "buy and hold" investing!

The Mississippi Bubble in Perspective

I have always believed that history—and particularly economic and market history—tends to follow long cycles. For this reason I find a lot of value in reading economic history books. One well-researched economic history book can add clarity that can get lost in the daily barrage of newspaper and magazine articles. Once in a while, a real gem that is both insightful and eminently readable rises to the top. I would put Niall Ferguson's recent book in that category. *The Ascent of Money: A Financial History of the World* is exactly what it claims to be. It is a comprehensive history of the development and rise of the financial industry and its impact on the world. As Ferguson writes,

> Behind each great historical phenomenon there lies a financial secret, and this book sets out to illuminate the most important of these. For example, the Renaissance created such a boom in the market for art and architecture because Italian bankers like the Medici made fortunes by applying Oriental mathematics to money [starting as far back as 1202 with the publication of Fibonacci's *Liber Abaci* and climaxing in the high Renaissance of the 1500s]. The Dutch Republic prevailed over the Habsburg Empire because having the world's first modern stock market was financially preferable to having the world's biggest silver mine [in the Dutch independence wars from 1568-1648]. **The problems of the French monarchy could not be resolved without a revolution because a convicted Scots murderer had wrecked the French financial system by unleashing the first stock market bubble and bust [in 1719-1720].** It was Nathan Rothschild [and his bond trading] as much as the Duke of Wellington who defeated Napoleon at Waterloo [in 1815].

Financial history is a long recurring cycle in which power shifts back and forth from creditors to debtors. The same can be said of the cyclical nature of the reputation of financiers, a.k.a. bankers. During boom times, they are viewed as providential stewards of prosperity, but during busts they are vilified and hunted down.

In his study of financial bubbles over the centuries, Ferguson identifies five typical stages:[11]

- *Displacement:* Some change in economic circumstances creates new and profitable opportunities for certain companies.
- *Euphoria* or overtrading: A feedback process sets in whereby rising expected profits lead to rapid growth in share prices.

- ***Mania* or bubble:** The prospect of easy capital gains attracts first-time investors and swindlers eager to bilk them of their money.
- ***Distress***: The insiders discern that expected profits cannot possibly justify the now exorbitant price of the shares and begin to take profits by selling.
- ***Revulsion* or discredit:** As share prices fall, the outsiders all stampede for the exits, causing the bubble to burst altogether

Though the focus of Ferguson's analysis was the stock market, the same insights would hold true in the housing and mortgage bubble and burst. "Revulsion" and "discredit" are words that aptly describe public views of investment real estate, mortgage lending and the financial sector in general.

Of course, it could be worse. The boom and subsequent bust that has caused so much misery today is nothing compared to aftermath of the Mississippi debacle.

The crash of the Mississippi bubble brought with it a period of prolonged deflationary weakness, as have *all* major bubbles in history. As a recent example, in the wake of the Internet bubble and bust we did *not* see large-scale consumer or producer price deflation, but we *did* see severe deflation in the areas most directly affected, namely technology and telecom hardware. As Thomas Friedman explained in *The World Is Flat*, the massive price deflation in fiber optic communications is what made the boom in Indian outsourcing and high-tech globalization possible.

It is during the long, post-boom cooling period in which the excesses of the prior boom are worked off. And this is the most important point that we would take from Ferguson's book. Niall Ferguson is one of the few economic commentators who shares my view that deflation, not inflation, will be the threat going forward—and specifically, asset deflation (as opposed to consumer price deflation). I do expect the Fed to try their damnedest to create inflation, and they will probably be successful, at least for a while, in some pockets of the commodities markets. In these cases, commodities cost more because the dollar depreciates and commodity prices rise. However asset inflation in big ticket items like real estate will prove dangerously elusive, and that is a big problem for homeowners and investors.

So, what does this mean for our current situation? While I would expect continued deflation in the housing sector for years to come, there will likely be some residual benefits. The oversupply of housing will mean that young families in the years ahead will get phenomenal bargains on their homes, values perhaps not enjoyed in a generation. In fact, deflation is a common thread throughout all past end-of-cycle economic busts. Without deflation at some point, the next generation could simply not afford to live. Although painful, it is a necessary evil.

But to repeat, I would view any increase in the inflation rate in the months ahead as being temporary noise. As the history of bubbles has proven, it is deflation that accompanies a bust, not inflation. And the broader the scope of the bubble, the more likely it is that deflation spreads to consumer prices in general. The government can and will fight it tooth and nail, but there is little they will be able to do about it in the end.

What lessons can we learn from this? One point on which nearly all market historians would agree is that **the bigger the bubble, the bigger the bust that follows**. Bubbles almost always return to the level at which they started. This was the case in the Mississippi Scheme—the share price rose from 500 livres to over 10,000 livres before collapsing back to 500—and it will likely be the case in the American real estate markets most affected by the bubble of the mid-2000s. It's *not* different this time.

Perhaps the most important lesson would be that **credit-fueled bubbles always end badly**. This was certainly the case with the spectacular collapse of the Japanese "miracle economy" at the beginning of the 1990s and the U.S. housing bubble—which led to the destruction of the banking system.

It is popular these days to lay all blame at the feet of the Fed for keeping interest rates artificially low. In the U.S. housing bubble, this is not really accurate or fair. The Fed played its part, of course, but so did irresponsible bankers, mortgage brokers, real estate agents, and even the home buyers themselves. As the baby boomers began to age and cut back their spending on housing in the mid-2000s, the financiers came up with more and more creative ways to extend credit to make up for the loss of natural consumer demand. If fewer people were interested in buying, better give those who *were* interested more credit to make up the difference. During boom times, everyone becomes punch drunk with self-indulgence if not outright greed, believing this time is different. What we know is, it most certainly was not!

The Fed's actions in the aftermath of the bust generated the most controversy. The Fed is now the biggest holder of U.S. Treasury debt. The Fed has always engaged in "open market operations," buying and selling U.S. government securities in an attempt to regulate the money supply. But this has evolved from a purely monetary objective to becoming a de facto funding mechanism for the U.S. government. The government is effectively printing money at the Fed in order to lend it to itself when the Fed uses that money to buy bonds that it will likely never sell. Though not quite as egregious as the Mississippi Scheme, whereby money was printed to buy inflated shares, there are obvious parallels.

Not too shockingly, this has given credence to "gold bug" hyperinflationary views that have been in the closet since the end of the 1970s. The gold bugs have been wrong in the sense that the inflation they feared has not yet materialized (and likely never will for demographic and deleveraging reasons we've discussed). But their fears were enough to send gold to new all-time highs.

The question on everyone's minds is "what happens when the Fed eventually has to reverse course?" When the Fed takes the punchbowl away, bond yields *should* rise and most risky assets—like stocks—*should* fall. But when? And by how much?

The volatile stock correction that started in late spring 2010 coincided with a lull in the Fed's easing. Given that stocks have had an unusually good run in the following months, we might expect a similar decline once the effects of QE2 wear off.

Regardless, we should learn from the lessons of history. Quantitative easing is dangerous and does not "fix" a bad economy. It does, however, generally lead to destabilizing asset bubbles. The quantitative easing following the "dot com" bust helped to create the conditions that made the housing and mortgage bubble possible. And today, rather than fix the root causes of the financial crises, yet another bubble is being formed, and you had better know how to play with bubbles. Most recently we have seen incipient bubbles in gold and food prices forming. Again, using history as a guide, the most likely outcome is a prolonged period of deflationary conditions and tepid growth.

# Chapter 6:

# What Really Drives the Economy

Regardless of what the stock market is doing, the economy is stuck in a rut. Signs of the current malaise are everywhere to be seen. Two, three or even four percent GDP growth is suddenly something to get excited about. Unemployment remains stubbornly close to 10% and consumer demand continues to be tepid at best. Business and bank failures have slowed—for now—but with lending standards forced as high as they currently are, new start-ups are withering on the vine for lack of investment capital. Sentiment among consumers remains sour. Frankly, it's ugly out there.

Should the government "do something" to get us out of this mess?

In fact, the government has already "done" quite a bit, running record budget deficits in recent years in its efforts to stimulate the economy. This deficit spending and the Fed's massive expansion of the monetary base have perhaps prevented the economy from falling harder than it already has, but no one in their right mind would argue that these actions have "fixed" what is broken. The truth is, the government *can't* fix what is broken. It's not big or powerful enough to do so, and frankly, we wouldn't *want* it to be.

To get an idea of what I'm talking about, take a look at Figure 6.1. Government spending—and this includes federal, state, and local governments—accounts for only 20.5% of the economy, as measured by gross domestic product (GDP). Gross private domestic investments—which includes everything from business software expenses to the houses we live in—chips in another 12.6%. Net exports—which is negative because we have a trade deficit—contributes -3.7%.

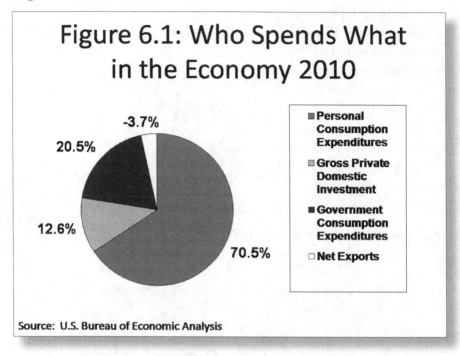

Source: U.S. Bureau of Economic Analysis

Consumer spending, at 70.5%, completely dominates the economy. It is not Fed Chairman Ben Bernanke who controls the economy but Homer Simpson. Yes, Ben Bernanke probably has more power over the economy than any other single person with the power of Federal Reserve monetary policy at his disposal. But collectively, it is the Homer and Marge Simpsons of the world that make the modern consumer-based economy go. This is an important point to remember and one that I will return to shortly.

Remember the Days…

Over the past decade, I've watched the media make a transformation. The 1990s were the decade of the "Money Honey," as CNBC correspondent Maria Bartiromo was known by her mostly male viewers in the investment world. In the sunny optimism of that decade, it was only appropriate to have an attractive, smiling young woman delivering the news.

But in today's media, we have a very different ambiance. Ms. Bartiromo is still around, but her style is markedly different. The smile has been replaced by cynicism. And perhaps most tellingly, Ms. Bartiromo herself is less of a media figure than she used to be. Today, reflecting the mood of the times, the news is more often delivered by the somber, scowling likes of Glenn Beck.

I mention Glenn Beck because I have heard him say, with righteous indignation, that "runaway" consumer spending was bankrupting the country. But is this statement remotely accurate? Has America really become a country of degenerate spendthrifts? Looking at Figure 6.1, I can understand why you might say yes. But the historical facts do not support this view at all.

Figure 6.2: Composition of U.S. Gross Domestic Product

■ Government consumption expenditures
□ Net exports of goods and services
▨ Gross private domestic investment
■ Personal consumption expenditures

Source: U.S. Bureau of Economic Analysis

Take a look at Figure 6.2, which tracks the components of Figure 6.1 historically. As you can see from even a quick look, consumer spending was often much higher than 70% in past decades. It fell to less than half of GDP during World War II, which is understandable. The entire American economy was on war footing at the time, and a large percentage of male would-be consumers were driving tanks in Europe and Asia. After the war, government spending and investment both remained higher than in past decades. Again, this stands to reason. The modern welfare state, for better or worse, was born in the 1930s and came of age in the 1940s and 1950s. Investment spending was also turbocharged by the building of America's suburbs as the GIs came home and started large families in what we now call the Baby Boom. This was also the period that saw the construction of America's largest and most significant public works project in history: the Interstate Highway System.

The recent surge in government spending notwithstanding, government expenditures and investment spending have been in decline, falling as a percentage of GDP, and consumer spending has grown to fill the void. Why anyone would consider this bad news is beyond me. This is *great* news. Adam Smith, the father of economics, said so himself in *The Wealth of Nations: "Consumption is the sole end and purpose of all production."*12

Unfortunately, this means that stimulus spending from Washington is unlikely to have much of an effect other than to stretch an already busted budget. Similar programs didn't work in Japan, and there is no reason to believe they will work here. I do understand there are massive differences between the United States and Japan. The most important is that the Japanese do not have a sizable generation waiting in the wings to make up for the aging Baby Boomer generation, while the United States does in the Echo Boomers, which are the kids of the Baby Boomers. However, those kids are still several years away from being able to spend at the level of their parents.

No, it's *not* different this time. In a modern consumer economy, stimulus spending doesn't work because it *can't*. Period.

## All About Consumer Spending

So, we've established that consumer spending is the 800 pound gorilla in the U.S. economy. As goes the consumer, so goes the economy.

The good news is that this makes the economy highly predictable. The bad news is that demographic trends suggest the American consumer may be in for several years of sluggish spending.

You have heard me mention Harry Dent before, and in this section I want to explain his demographic research and its implications for the consumer and, by proxy, the economy. Harry Dent brought to the world of financial and investment research the insights that marketers have used since the dawn of capitalism: **consumer spending decisions are driven largely by age and stage of life** (see Figure 6.3).

# Figure 6.3: Spending By Stage of Life

| 18-22 Single | 22-30 Young Married | 31-42 Young Family | 46-50 Family, College Kids | 50+ Empty Nesters | 60+ Retired |

Source: HS Dent Foundation (HSDent.com)

Academic economists have touched on this theme to an extent. Like many things in modern economics, it started with John Maynard Keynes. Lord Keynes gets a bad rap today, and to be fair much of it is deserved. Virtually every government in the world has rather cynically used Keynes's work to justify irresponsible deficit spending in the name of "economic stimulus." Somehow, they never seem to get to the part of Keynes's work that talks about running budget surpluses when the economy is booming in order to pay down the debts incurred from deficit spending when times were hard. Funny how *that* works. But while these aspects of Keynes's work tend to generate a lot of controversy, much of his lesser-known work is quite insightful. Keynes was a bright guy, even if the views for which he is most famous have been soundly discredited in the decades since his passing.

Prior to Keynes, most economic theory was focused on production, or the supply side of the equation. Consumption, driven by end-user demand, was merely an afterthought, something that just "happened" and didn't need to be explained. This was best summarized by Say's Law,[13] a maxim memorized by every freshman economics student: **"Supply creates its own demand."**

During the pits of the Great Depression, Keynes asked what should have been an obvious question: what if it *doesn't?* What if demand doesn't just "happen" as a result of the production process? What if workers opt to save their paychecks rather than spend them? What if the system, as we have grown accustomed to it, breaks down?

To answer these questions, Keynes built a simple model to explain consumer behavior (allow me to be technical here for just a minute):

$$C = c_0 + c_1 Y^d$$

where

$c_0$ = baseline consumption on necessities; what we must spend to survive.

$c_1$ = marginal propensity to consume, or the percentage of your income that you chose to spend

$Y^d$ = income

In plain English, this means that our total spending (C) is equal to our spending on necessities ($c_0$) plus the percentage of our incomes that we spend on non-essentials ($c_1 Y^d$). Easy enough.

Unfortunately, this model is a little too simple. Keynes fails to note that spending and saving habits are affected by level of wealth or by age and stage of life. The same person will have a very different "marginal propensity to consume" at different points in his or her life. When we are in our early 40s, for example, we generally spend quite a bit more freely than we do at 70, when we are presumably retired and living off of our investments!

Keynes deserves credit for being the first person to approach consumption scientifically, but it is obvious that his model was incomplete and not reflective of the real world. Many of these deficiencies were addressed by the economists Modigliani, Brumberg, and Ando in the 1950s and 60s in what became known as the Life Cycle Hypothesis (Figure 6.4).

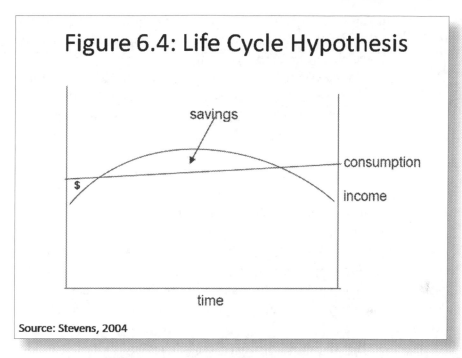

# Figure 6.4: Life Cycle Hypothesis

savings

consumption

income

$

time

Source: Stevens, 2004

These economists graphically displayed what every household intuitively knows. People follow a life cycle of earning and spending. In the early stages of our careers, our incomes are low relative to our expenses, often forcing us to take out large debts for homes, cars, appliances, etc. In middle age, we earn enough money to meet all of our current expenses, plus save for retirement. And naturally, in retirement our income falls and we slowly spend down our savings. Makes sense.

This model, though more advanced than Keynes's, is still problematic. Notice that income makes a curve while consumption makes a straight line. This chart is suggesting that our consumer spending increases in a mild, linear fashion from birth until death. I'll get into why that's not an accurate representation shortly.

In 1957, the great economist Milton Friedman made his own modifications to the Consumption Function and to the Life Cycle Hypothesis and dubbed it the "Permanent Income Hypothesis." Friedman's idea was this: people base their consumer spending on what they consider their "permanent" income, or their average income over time. They do this in an attempt to maintain a relatively constant standard of living, even though their incomes may vary wildly over time and particularly as they age. We don't shop at Saks Fifth Avenue one day and then at Goodwill the next because we had a single bad pay period. Our lifestyle remains more or less constant, even as income fluctuates.

This goes a long way to explaining why Americans love consumer debt as much as they do. It's ok to spend more than you make today, because your salary will be high enough after that next promotion to pay it all back.

Keynes's model, remember, assumed that people spend a constant proportion of their current incomes. Friedman assumes that people are forward-looking and base consumption decisions today on income expectations for tomorrow. Changes in current income, if perceived to be temporary, have little effect on spending. Friedman correctly realized that a family's standard of living is "sticky." When dad's bonus check is a little disappointing one year, the family does not instantly eschew Cadillac in favor of Chevrolet. Whether for pride, concern for their children, or simple inertia, Americans are slow to ratchet down their lifestyles.

Friedman's model, though interesting, is also deeply flawed. Like the Life Cycle models, it assumes that spending rises indefinitely into the future. Intuitively, we all know this isn't true. As we age, we become far more conservative in our spending habits. This is partially out of economic necessity, in that most Americans live on a fixed income in retirement from Social Security, annuities, bonds, or pension payments and their budget must fit within those means. But perhaps even more important than this natural conservatism that comes with age is the fact that, at some point, we have already *made* all of life's major purchases. We tend to drive less as we age, meaning that we replace our cars less often. We already own the largest and most expensive home we are likely to ever live in, and we have already stuffed it full of furniture and appliances. Apart from basic necessities and leisure activities, there is simply not that much to spend our money on!

## Figure 6.5: Household Spending By Age

Source: Consumer Expenditure Survey

## Figure 6.6: HS Dent Modified Life Cycle Hypothesis

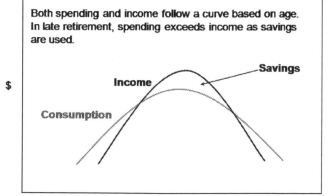

Both spending and income follow a curve based on age. In late retirement, spending exceeds income as savings are used.

Source: HS Dent Foundation

While we know all of this intuitively, it is nice to be able to back it up with hard statistics. Using data from the U.S. Consumer Expenditure Survey, we see that consumer spending is largely a function of age (Figure 6.5). We spend increasingly more raising our families until our late 40s or early 50s, after which time we pare down our spending and save for retirement. Consider Figure 6.6. In this case, the income line has the same basic shape as in Figure 6.4, though the consumption line has been transformed into a curve, like Figure 6.5 would suggest.

With this insight, I'd like to get into the meat of this research. What is true of the individual is also true of the country as a whole. Entire generations follow this HS Dent Modified Life Cycle, accumulating debts to buy cars, homes, and perhaps education for their children, and then paying off these debts to save for retirement. The Baby Boomers—the biggest and richest generation in history—are now entering the tail end of this cycle. The Boomers are now at a stage of their lives where it no longer makes sense to take on new debts. They are deleveraging, paying off their debts, for two critical reasons:

1.  It is a natural cycle.
2.  Because they have to!

An over-indebted, over-leveraged population always occurs at the bottom of economic cycles, but not typically as bad as this one. As an example of excess, never before have people without money or a source of income been able to borrow to buy a home in which there is no possible way for them to pay it back. This is a big reason why I see deflation persisting for much longer than most economists think.

Do you think this sounds too simplistic? I can assure you that, yes, it really *is* that simple. I'll start from the basics and build my case. The demographic argument is compelling, and most of my clients instinctively get it when I explain it to them. Armed with this information, I wrote my special report: **An Economic Tsunami Lies Ahead – *How to Prepare for This Perfect Storm*** (see Appendix A), which forecasted and predicted the current economic malaise we are currently in and subsequent stock market crash.

Figure 6.7: Immigration Adjusted Birth Index

Source: HS Dent Foundation

Let's start at the beginning—with births. The U.S. National Center for Health Statistics tracks the number of babies born every year. To account for immigrants who were not born here, we add the number of immigrants by their birth year to the U.S. numbers. This gives us the Immigration-Adjusted Birth Index (Figure 6.7), which was first developed by Harry Dent.

This is where the analysis gets interesting. If we know how many Americans we have by birth year and we know at what age they tend to buy something, we suddenly have a very powerful forecasting tool.

As an example, let's consider an example near and dear to parents and grandparents: college education. Take a look at Figure 6.9, which is a close-up of the circled area in Figure 6.8 with an important twist. In Figure 6.9, we push the circled portion of Figure 6.8 forward by 18 years to account for the age that most kids go to college.

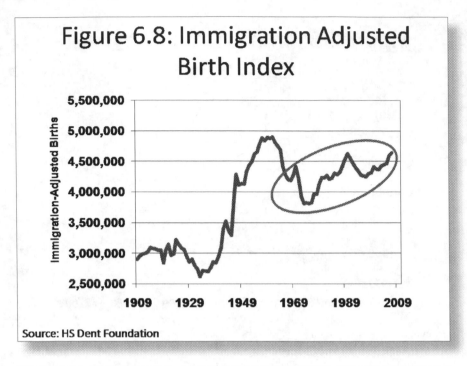

Figure 6.8: Immigration Adjusted Birth Index

Source: HS Dent Foundation

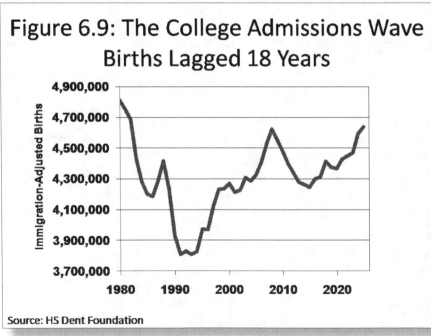

Figure 6.9: The College Admissions Wave Births Lagged 18 Years

Source: HS Dent Foundation

Have you ever noticed how competitive it is to get into a good school these days? And how expensive too, for that matter? When I was looking at universities as a young man, having a decent set of high school grades and perhaps having an extracurricular activity or two was more than sufficient to get into a good school. These days, a kid has to have a 4.0+ GPA, be a concert-caliber musician, throw a football like a Heisman candidate and spend a summer feeding homeless children in India to even be considered. After looking at Figure 6.9, you can see why. The huge generation that is made of up the children of the Baby Boomers—the Echo Boomers—has been busting the capacity of America's universities. The demand for college education has far outstripped supply, causing competition for admission slots and tuition expenses to soar.

Yes, it is simple economics. When demand is higher than supply, prices rise. In the case of college admissions, the "price" is both monetary and merit-based, in the form of higher test scores and admissions standards.

Interestingly, demographic trends suggest that this trend will reverse, at least for a few years. Take a look at Figure 6.10, which zooms in a little closer on Figure 6.9. The number of 18-year-olds coming down the pipeline peaked in 2008 and will continue falling until 2015. This means that, all else being equal, kids applying for colleges over the next five years should have an easier go at it.

Mark my words: at some point over the next five years, you will see a pundit on TV bemoaning the fact that "standards at American universities are falling...average test scores are falling... What has happened to our youth?"

When you hear this you will know the real reason why. It won't be because American children are getting dumber, but rather a case of simple arithmetic. Colleges have massively expanded their facilities just as there are fewer students to use them. Standards will have to fall in order to fill up the empty seats!

Getting back into consumer spending, we know that Americans tend to peak in their consumer spending at around age 48. Applying this insight to the same methodology we used above, we get one of the most powerful predictors ever invented, the *Spending Wave* (Figure 6.11), also developed by Harry Dent.

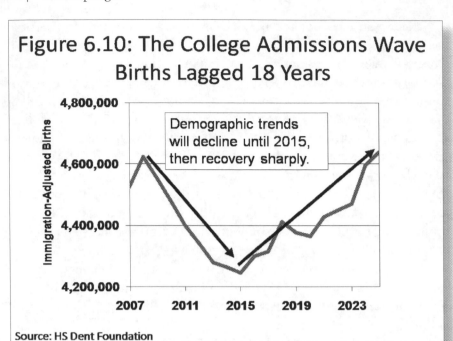

Figure 6.10: The College Admissions Wave
Births Lagged 18 Years

Demographic trends will decline until 2015, then recovery sharply.

Source: HS Dent Foundation

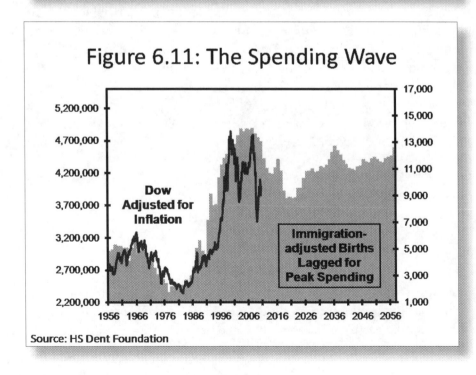

Figure 6.11: The Spending Wave

Dow Adjusted for Inflation

Immigration-adjusted Births Lagged for Peak Spending

Source: HS Dent Foundation

The Spending Wave is one of the most useful tools in demographic research. As you can see in Figure 6.11, the Dow Jones Industrial Average adjusted for inflation had a strong resemblance to the Immigration-Adjusted Birth Index. When you lag the Birth Index by 48 years to account for the average age of peak spending, the two charts move together uncannily.

Again, intuitively, this makes a lot of sense. As I mentioned above, it is the Homer and Marge Simpsons that drive 70% of the U.S. economy. Over the long-term, the stock market's movement is a reflection of economic growth. So, over very long-term periods, demographic trends should have a significant impact on stock prices.

Demographic trends most certainly do *not* determine what the day-to-day fluctuations of the market will be. In the short-term, "noise" factors and current events have a far greater impact. Demographic trends do not necessarily pinpoint market meltdowns, such as the one in late 2008 that was ignited by the Lehman Brothers failure.

As the market has become more volatile in recent years, the neat, clean correlation on the Spending Wave has gotten a little more jagged. The point of the chart, however, is still very obvious: demographic trends suggest that stock returns will be disappointing in the years ahead. The Dow may or may not continue the downward track projected by the Spending Wave; only time will tell. But suffice it to say, the fantastic returns that we all got used to in the 1980s and 1990s are likely a thing of the past for at least the foreseeable future,

During the decade of the 2000s, the market returned almost exactly nothing. That's ten years with no portfolio gains to show for it. Granted, stocks started the decade of the 2000s at ridiculously high valuations, and those excesses needed time to be worked off. Now, in 2010, stock valuations are far more attractive than in 2000. So, it is certainly possible that, despite the negative demographic trends and the continued menace of debt deflation, stocks could enjoy positive returns in the years ahead because much of this bad news is already factored into current prices. Still, given the risks, this is clearly not a time to throw caution to the wind with *your* hard-earned retirement dollars.

Attention, Demographics and the Stock Market

In 2005, Stefano DellaVigna and Joshua Pollet published one of the most insightful papers in the history of academic finance: "Attention, Demographics, and the Stock Market."[14] DellaVigna and Pollet wrote,

> We consider the case of demographic information. Cohort size fluctuations produce forecastable demand changes for age-sensitive sectors, such as toys, bicycles, beer, life insurance, and nursing homes. These demand changes are predictable once a specific cohort is born.

What the professors are saying is that demographic information can be used to predict the demand for certain products. Consider college dorm rooms. Allowing for changes in the percentage of kids attending college, school administrators can budget their need for dorm rooms eighteen years in advance. A surge in births today means a surge in demand for dorm beds eighteen years from now, and a slowdown in births today means a slowdown in demand for dorm beds. This same logic can be applied to stock market sectors as well. As the professors continue,

> We use lagged consumption and demographic data to forecast future consumption demand growth induced by changes in age structure. We find that demand forecasts predict profitability by industry. Moreover, forecasted demand changes 5 to 10 years in the future predict annual industry stock returns. **One additional percentage point of annualized demand growth due to demographics predicts a 5 to 10 percentage point increase in annual abnormal industry stock returns**. However, forecasted demand changes over shorter horizons do not predict stock returns.

This last point—that demographic analysis works better over longer time horizons—makes a lot of sense when you consider that the average holding period for stocks is less than a year. Investors, both professional and amateur, are known to be "myopic" in their behavior. They look at quarterly earnings per share growth, or if they are technicians, they look at what the stock price is doing *today*.

Demographic trends are slow moving and, frankly, boring. The frenetic bustle you see on CNBC is *sexy*. But demographics? Yeah, not so much.

But herein lies our opportunity. **If we have the patience to assemble a solid portfolio of strong investments supported by durable demographic trends, we can quietly post good returns without being distracted by the noise.**

DellaVigna and Pollet conclude that the demographic model works better for industries with "higher barriers to entry and with more pronounced age patterns in consumption." This only stands to reason. High barriers to entry prevent new Johnny-come-lately companies from quickly jumping in to satisfy excess, demographic-driven demand. It also makes sense that it works better for products with pronounced age patterns. Demographics can tell you how much demand there will be for artificial knees or nursing homes. But they're not going to tell you a lot about demand for General Electric aircraft engines.

This brings a new element to the use of demographics as an investment tool. Not only can demographic trends be used from a "macro" perspective, but from a "micro" perspective as well to identify promising companies and sectors. Of course, these insights are not limited to passive portfolio investors. Successful entrepreneurs can and do use it every day.

Entrepreneurs often have a better idea of what's happening in the real economy than portfolio managers. It only makes sense; while a portfolio manager can easily get lost in the world of abstract financial jargon, a successful entrepreneur has to roll up his sleeves and work in the real world. As investors, we would likely be more successful in our stock picking if we approached the process with an entrepreneur's mindset.

Several months ago, I was delighted to see that the *Financial Times* reported on a pair of young entrepreneurs who have built a successful retailing business following these same principles.[15]

In 2005 Marc Lore and Vinit Bharara launched **Diapers.com**, an e-commerce site selling diapers and other baby products.

**"We came across the baby market,"** the *Financial Times* quotes Mr. Lore. **"It was a $40bn market and incredibly fragmented online, with lots of players but no number-one brand.** So we thought: 'We need to build a brand, and not do it by beating rivals on keyword marketing [to attract internet searches].'"

In its five years of existence, Diapers.com has become a $275 million business and a top "pure play" e-commerce site not associated with a traditional retailer. The owners claim the site has become the biggest online seller of infant car seats and that it sells four times as many diapers as Amazon.com. Not a bad track record!

With live births still near record highs in the United States, Lore and Bharara are in the right place at the right time, and I expect their business to do well in the coming years. The family formation of the Echo Boomers should be a steady source of profits for companies like diapers.com for quite some time.

Meanwhile, an old familiar retail face is back with a vengeance. After being taken private in 2005 by a group of investors, **Toys R Us** announced in May 2010 that it plans to go public again through an $800 million initial public offering. The stock will trade on the New York Stock Exchange under the ticker symbol "TOYS."

Toys R Us fell on hard times in the late 1990s and early 2000s as it faced stiff competition from discounters like Wal-Mart and Target and from Internet retailers. The company was painfully slow to adopt the Internet as a major sales channel, but **bad demographics also played a role**. The number of American births went into a sharp decline in 1990 and did not reach a bottom until 1997. Fewer babies meant fewer children a few years later—and fewer parents buying expensive toys.

Not surprisingly, the recovery in the birth rate in the late 1990s and throughout the 2000s has been a boon to Toys R Us.

Of course, demographic analysis can also be used on toys of a more mature nature. Sales of large cruising motorcycles are almost entirely driven by demographic trends. And unfortunately, the news just doesn't get better for Harley-Davidson and its peers in the "big bike" business. U.S. motorcycle sales shrank by 14.1% in the third quarter of 2010 from the year before, extending the grueling decline to 15 consecutive quarters. Remember, that is a 14.1% decline from the already *deeply* depressed sales figures of 2009.

According to the *Financial Times*, "Sales are now less than half the level at the peak of the market in 2006... Highway bike sales totaled 383,000 last year, down from 660,000 in 2008 and 724,000 in 2007."[16]

How bad is it? Some of Harley's Japanese competitors did not produce 2010 models.

I can't help but feel sorry for the company. You cannot say that Harley's woes are due to bad management. Harley's management team generally gets high marks. No, Harley-Davidson's problem is **bad demographics**.

Harley's big bikes are a product purchased almost exclusively by white males in their mid-to-late 40s. All of this was well and good ten years ago when the Baby Boomers first began to enter this demographic sweet spot. Harley never had it better. The largest generation in history had just become their best customer.

Unfortunately, those days are gone. The Boomer male has passed this stage and has likely shaved off the goatee and closeted the leather jacket. Good luck selling the bike used, though. Used bike prices have plummeted in recent years as inventories have built up.

Try as Harley might to reach out to other demographic consumer groups—younger and non-Caucasian men and women, for example—Harley's future has already been written. Sales of the company's iconic bikes should continue to disappoint investors for the foreseeable future, barring the occasional surprise.

Across the Atlantic, changing demographics are wreaking havoc on another iconic industry—German beer.

Normally it's not considered politically correct to play on national stereotypes, but the Germans themselves have cultivated a macho image as a nation that knows how to knock back a stein or two. Visiting a proper Bavarian biergarten and ordering an obscenely large beer (from a barmaid with biceps big enough to beat most Harley bikers at arm wrestling) is practically a rite of passage for visitors to the country.

So, it might come as a surprise that German beer consumption is in a long-term decline. According to the *Economist*, German beer drinking has declined from 142 liters per person per year in 1991 to "only" 110 liters in 2009.[17]

That's still a lot of beer, mind you. Enough to put most Americans accustomed to watery Bud Light in the hospital. Still, that is a decline of more than a fifth.

As you might guess, demographics are the driving force behind this change. As the Economist explains, *"An ageing, shrinking population is drinking less... Even among the traditionally hard-boozing middle-aged, health concerns have curbed drinking."*

It's not just German beer consumption that is suffering in Europe, however. The incoming Dutch government is considering strict new regulation of Amsterdam's cannabis cafes and red light district. The moves would significantly shrink the red light district and could end up putting the iconic cannabis cafes out of business altogether.

It appears that the Dutch—world famous for their socially liberal attitudes—are becoming significantly less tolerant as the years go by. As a simple measuring gauge, the number of cannabis cafes has halved since 1995, from roughly 1,400 to 700[18].

So, what is the story? Are the Dutch tired of being known as the world's pimps and drug dealers? Has the novelty simply worn off? What is making Dutch society become more socially conservative?

One obvious answer is that the Dutch are tired of seeing American and British youths making buffoons of themselves in their smoky cafes. The liberal policies regarding drugs and prostitution tend to attract the wrong kind of tourist. But there is a larger issue at play as well, and as you might guess, demographics are at the center of it. And I'm not talking about the influx of North African Muslim immigrants, which is a major issue these days in Dutch politics. No, I'm talking about the Dutch Baby Boomers.

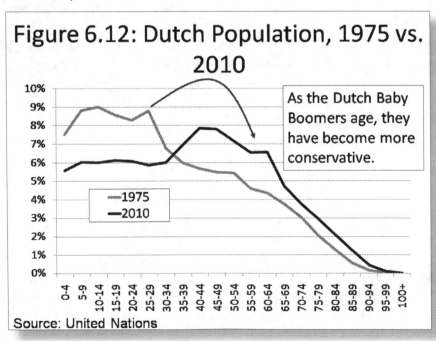

Figure 6.12: Dutch Population, 1975 vs. 2010

As the Dutch Baby Boomers age, they have become more conservative.

Source: United Nations

As you can see in the chart, the Netherlands was a young country in 1975. The Dutch Baby Boomers were teenagers and 20-somethings at that time.

Not surprisingly, the cannabis cafes became legal in 1976, when the Baby Boomers as a generation were in their prime years of misspent youth.

As the Boomers in both the United States and Europe have aged, they have maintained a fair bit of the personality of their younger years, a mixture of anti-establishment rebelliousness and wide-eyed idealism.

But in other ways, they have become their parents. In fact, in some ways they are far more strict. Boomer parents were notorious about coddling their children and micromanaging every aspect of their lives. Perhaps, remembering their own wilder years, they didn't trust their kids with the same amount of freedom that they themselves enjoyed.

The Boomers have also become wealthier as they have aged, and perhaps these bourgeois bohemians consider the seedy element associated with drugs and prostitution to be bad for property values.

I could write an entire book of nothing but demographic anecdotes like these, but I will spare you for now. With an understanding of this material, there are certainly attractive investment opportunities out there, and I'll get into my recommendations in a later chapter. But first, I want to dive into demographics from a different angle.

# Chapter 7:

# Demographics and the Stock Market

I'm not the first person to write about the effects of an aging society on stock prices, of course. In certain financial circles demographics have gotten downright trendy. In the last chapter, I mentioned the groundbreaking work of DellaVigna, Pollet and Dent. Naturally, there are also other views, often conflicting, that I want to discuss in this chapter.

Professor Jeremy Siegel of the Wharton School of Business is one of the most respected minds in the world of investment research and for good reason. His *Stocks for the Long Run* is a solid piece of research that belongs on every investor's shelf. While Siegel can be dogmatic in his defense of equities (there seems to be no circumstance in which Siegel *wouldn't* recommend buying stocks), his work is top notch and should be taken seriously.

Unfortunately, I can't say the same for his demographic research. Professor Siegel, Fed Chairman Ben Bernanke and popular financial writer and speaker Robert Kiyosaki have all written about demographics in a similar way. For simplicity's sake, I'll lump them all together as "the Siegel view." At its roots, the Siegel view is a variation of the life cycle models I covered in the last chapter.

The San Francisco Federal Reserve Bank explored the Siegel view before Siegel himself. Cogley and Royer's 1998 paper "The Baby Boom, the Baby Bust, and Asset Markets" summarizes Siegel's basic model:

> To understand the relation between demography and capital markets, it is useful to think about the Life Cycle model of

consumption and saving. Roughly speaking, the Life Cycle model states that people work and save when they are young and live off the proceeds when they retire…. (See Figure 7.1)

[They] work until age 65, at which time they begin to sell off assets and live off the proceeds. The key feature… is that wealth has a hump shape over the life cycle. It peaks at retirement age and then begins to decline. **In other words, older people tend to be net sellers of financial assets.**

In an economy with a stable age distribution, this would have no effect on capital markets. When each cohort reached retirement age, it would sell its assets to younger cohorts who were accumulating wealth, and with steady population growth there would always be enough of the latter to absorb the sales of the former. But what happens when population growth isn't steady and the economy's age distribution isn't stable? **In particular, what happens when the old-age dependency ratio rises, and there are proportionally fewer young savers to buy up the assets of the older retirees?** In this case, by the law of supply and demand, one would expect the price of assets to fall. As aging baby boomers begin to sell their financial assets, they will presumably be selling to the next waves of savers, the so-called Generation Xers and Yers, which are significantly smaller population cohorts. With relatively fewer buyers than in the past, boomers may find themselves selling into a weak market when they retire.[19]

The problem with this argument is that is it so *close* to being correct. In a free economy, prices for everything are determined by supply and demand. Even in cases where prices are fixed, such as in rent-control policies and socialized medicine, the "price" finds a way to adjust to supply and demand. In cases like these where the dollar price is not allowed to fluctuate, prices adjust through mechanisms like rationing or waiting lists—a higher "price" is a longer wait.

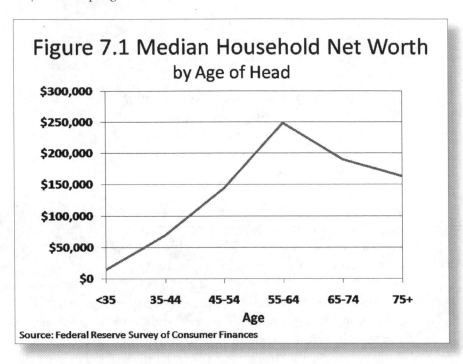

Figure 7.1 Median Household Net Worth by Age of Head

Source: Federal Reserve Survey of Consumer Finances

Figure 7.2: Share of U.S. Households Owning Stocks

Source: The State of Working America 2006/2007

Naturally, stocks are no exception. In fact, the stock market is as close to a "pure" free market as has ever existed, with prices changing almost instantly to reflect every infinitesimal shift in sentiment by traders. *Forbes* columnist Ken Fisher explores this idea in his delightfully irreverent book *The Only Three Things That Count*: "There are just two factors in this whole, wide, wonderful, and whacky world driving stock prices. Always and everywhere, stock prices are derived singularly by shifts in supply and demand…. These dueling pressures in supply and demand set prices of all we buy."

So, demand constantly shifts with the whims and emotions of traders, but what about the *supply* of stock? At any given time, the float of traded shares is relatively fixed. Sure, Bill Gates could massively increase the supply of Microsoft by dumping his personal holdings, but significant insider sales tend to be rare. And in this case, we are talking about *existing* shares being floated. What about new shares? What about entirely new companies going public?

"Shifts in supply are different," Fisher continues. "In the short run, the actual supply of securities is almost completely fixed as it takes time and effort and a cooperative multiplicity of players to create new shares or destroy existing ones. Think about how long IPOs or mergers need to evolve, and the amount of advance notice the companies are required by law to give the public."

Adding new supply is expensive, time-consuming, and depends on a lot of complex factors. As Fisher continues, "…no matter what anyone would have you believe, no one has any way to predict supply in the far distant future. This is among the reasons why long-term mechanical forecasting notions are usually way, way wide of the mark. No one knows what whacky things may happen to the creation or destruction of the supply of equities 5 to 20 years from now."

This is the flaw in the "supply side" of the Siegel demographic argument. In this modified Life Cycle theory, stock trading takes place within a closed "box." There is no consideration for new issues of stock, executive stock options, share buybacks or even mergers and bankruptcies.

There are failings in the demand side as well. This modified Life Cycle hypothesis assumes that rank and file Americans uniformly accumulate stocks throughout their working lives and then slowly sell them off in retirement. As Cogley and Royer discuss above, this is problematic because the large Boomer generation has no one to sell its holdings to.

As intuitive—and scary—as this explanation sounds, it doesn't hold up to a critical analysis. First, it rather "democratically" assumes that ownership of stock is dominated by rank-and-file Americans through their IRAs, 401ks and brokerage accounts. As an egalitarian society, this is how we prefer to view the world. Unfortunately, it is patently false. The stock market is not a one-man-one-vote democracy in which the little guy makes a difference; it is a plutocracy in which the "big money" dominates. Consider Figure 7.2. After decades of growing participation through vehicles such as retirement accounts, mutual funds and discounted brokerage accounts, more than half of Americans still hold no stock in any form. Even more telling, *only a third of households have stock holdings of over $5,000*. And remember, these numbers only go through the mid-2000s, which is as recent as reliable data was available. After the market meltdown of 2008, it is safe to assume the percentages are now lower.

But what about those Boomers who *do* own stocks? Even if a majority of Americans own no stock, might the selling by a large minority be significant enough to chop the market down a few notches? And wouldn't demographic trends suggest that this was likely?

Again, this explanation doesn't hold up to critical analysis. While Figure 7.2 indicates how many Americans own stocks, Figure 7.3 takes a closer look at those who do. It is immediately obvious that the overwhelming majority of stock market wealth is controlled by a small percentage of Americans. The top 5% wealthiest own a full 65% of the stock market. The top 0.05% alone controls more than a quarter! Meanwhile, 80% of the population (the 401ks and IRAs) holds less that 10% of the total.

The typical upper-middle-class Baby Boomer with a 401k balance of a couple hundred thousand dollars or even a million or two will most likely be selling stocks in his golden years to fund his living expenses. He will gradually shift mostly out of stocks and into income investments like bonds. Chances are good that the income alone won't be sufficient, so he will slowly spend down his principal as well. Or, he may opt to sell all of his stocks and bonds at once and buy an annuity. This is standard financial planning, and it is exactly what he should do. But as Figure 7.3 demonstrates, this periodic retirement selling is like a drop in the ocean. Bill Gates and Michael Dell won't be selling their stock holdings to fund retirement, and neither will the rest of the top 5% of stockholders that control 65% of the market. It is the middle class—the 80% of the population that owns less than 10% of the equity—that follows the Life Cycle Hypothesis, not the rich.

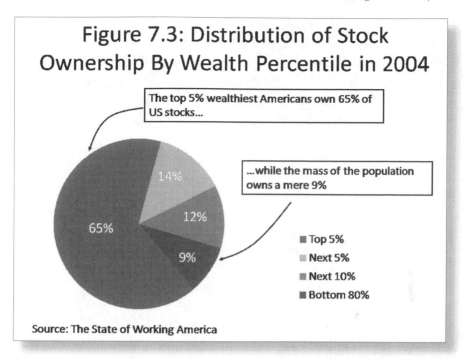

Figure 7.3: Distribution of Stock Ownership By Wealth Percentile in 2004

The top 5% wealthiest Americans own 65% of US stocks...

...while the mass of the population owns a mere 9%

- Top 5%
- Next 5%
- Next 10%
- Bottom 80%

Source: The State of Working America

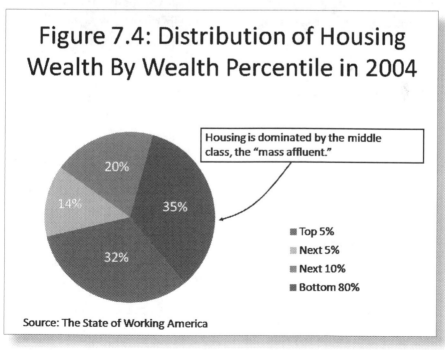

Figure 7.4: Distribution of Housing Wealth By Wealth Percentile in 2004

Housing is dominated by the middle class, the "mass affluent."

- Top 5%
- Next 5%
- Next 10%
- Bottom 80%

Source: The State of Working America

Even though the *stock market* is still dominated by the rich, the American *economy* is dominated by the middle class, the "mass affluent." A good way to illustrate this is to look at wealth tied to home ownership. As seen in Figure 7.4, the top 5% still owns a disproportionate share of the country's real estate. But the key here is that it is the bottom 80% that dominates, not the top tier.

The same holds true for the overall economy. It is the middle class that fills the aisles of Best Buy, Wal-Mart, and the Home Depot. It is the discretionary income of mainstream American that allows new Starbucks franchises to sprout up like weeds. And it is ultimately this same middle-class America that should cause stock market gains to be somewhat tepid going forward, but not for the same reasons that Jeremy Siegel and his contemporaries believe.

I said it before, and I'll say it again: Consumer spending drives economic growth. In the end, it's the only real reason we go to work in the morning. As the rank-and-file of the Baby Boomer generation passes its peak spending years, it will begin to curtail its spending and increase its savings. Less consumption means less need for production and retail. This means factory orders slow down. Fewer big-box stores get built. Fewer trucks are needed to transport fewer goods to fewer stores. This effect ripples throughout the economy—there is demand for fewer truck stops selling fewer energy drinks, packs of gum and embroidered trucker caps.

The Boomers' consumer spending has been the engine that makes this entire machine move. A decline in spending growth has a ripple effect that should lead to a slowdown in corporate profits—and ultimately a slower rate of return for stock prices. Thus, demographics can be used as a highly-effective forecasting tool, but doing so requires that you "connect the dots." The problem with the academic models used by Siegel and the Fed is that they are too simple. Supply and demand drive the market, but they ultimately do so based on investor expectations of future earnings. And demographics are the best long-term indicator for the direction of future earnings. This was the insight of DellaVigna and Pollet's research on individual stocks, and in my view, the correct way to understand the effect of demographics on stock prices.

Speaking of prices, I'm dedicating one last chapter to demographics. I will explore how *people*, not just monetary policy, affect the rate of inflation.

# Chapter 8:

# Demographics and Prices

In Chapter 2, I discussed the basic mechanics of inflation and deflation with an emphasis on the recent financial crisis. In this chapter we will discuss various views of what drives changes in prices. Most views have at least some truth to them, but it is the demographic view that is the most compelling and relevant today. If inflation and deflation are common themes in this book, it is because I consider them to be extraordinarily important to us as investors. The portfolio you should build for deflationary times is very different from one you should build for inflationary times, and making the wrong choice can cost you dearly. In deflationary times, assets that produce safe, predictable *income* are generally best. This would include bonds, preferred stock, certain annuity products and even high-quality dividend-paying blue chip stocks in some cases. But in an inflationary environment, these kinds of assets get absolutely killed. If the cost of living rises due to inflation but your investment income does not, you get poorer every day. In an inflationary time, hard assets like gold, commodities, and real estate generally do best. But as you can imagine, during deflationary times when prices are falling, these kinds of assets are the last thing you want to own. Investors who loaded up on gold and silver during the inflationary 1970s saw much of their wealth evaporate during the 1980s, when inflation fell.

With all of this in mind, let's jump into our discussion on the root causes of price changes.

There are two main schools of thought, Keynesian and Monetarist, pioneered by John Maynard Keynes and Milton Friedman, respectively.

Other, less orthodox views have used demographics to explain inflation and deflation. Thus far, the best demographic arguments have been made by David Hackett Fischer and Gregory Clark for pre-industrial economies and by Harry S. Dent, Jr. for post-industrial, mass-affluent societies like ours today. Fed Chairman Ben Bernanke and Professor Jeremy Siegel—whom we mentioned in the last chapter—also offered some insights on the matter, and their views will be discussed. We'll examine each of these views in the pages that follow.

In Chapter 2, the charts I used to describe "good deflation," "bad deflation," and "demand-based inflation" were straight out of the Keynesian textbook (See Figures 2.2, 2.3 and 2.5). Demand-based inflation is called "demand-pull" inflation by Keynesians, but the gist is the same. When increases in aggregate demand (due to increased private and government spending) outstrip increases in aggregate supply, prices rise. It's exactly like an auction. Prices rise when there are more bidders for a given item. And of course, the opposite is also true: prices fall when there are fewer bidders.

The other form of inflation that Keynesians identify is "cost-push" inflation, also called "supply shock" inflation. For those who remember the gas shortages of the 1970s, that is what we are talking about here. Prices rise when there is a sudden disruption in supply that causes an unexpected shortage. This form of inflation tends to be the most destructive to the health of the economy, and thankfully it is relatively rare.

Either form of inflation can lead to what Keynes called the "price/wage spiral" in which workers get used to rising prices and thus demand higher wages. Of course, rising labor costs force companies to raise their prices further, creating a vicious cycle that can be difficult to break. This was the situation in the late 1970s. It took some of the most hawkish Fed action in history under Paul Volker and two deep recessions in the early 1980s to finally break it.

The other mainstream view of inflation and deflation is that of the Monetarist school, led by the late Milton Friedman. Friedman proposed that changes in the price level are almost purely effects of monetary policy by the Federal Reserve. One of Friedman's most quoted statements was: *"Inflation is always and everywhere a monetary phenomenon."* In this line of thinking, if the Fed "prints" more money than is needed to make the economy function, the value of that money decreases and the price of everything rises. Hence, we have inflation. On the flip side, if the Fed fails to print enough money, we have a "shortage" of cash, and prices fall: deflation. This is loosely the view of Fed Chairman Ben Bernanke and his predecessor Alan Greenspan, and there is definitely some truth to it. Central banks are certainly capable of creating artificial inflation or deflation. It wasn't that long ago that Brazil had an inflation rate of over 1,000% per year, and when referring to U.S. economic history both Friedman and Bernanke have mentioned that unnecessarily high interest rates by the Fed were a major contributing factor to the deflation of the Great Depression. Central banks can get monetary policy wrong in either direction, causing inflation or deflation as the case might be.

Friedman is correct to say that a central bank *can* affect the money supply. But his theory has one very large hole in it. A central bank *cannot* increase the *velocity* of money, or the frequency with which a dollar changes hands in the economy. As Keynes correctly pointed out, in the absence of underlying demand, stimulative monetary policy (a.k.a. printing more money) is akin to "pushing on a string." Simply having more money around does not guarantee that it will be spent.

## Demographics: The Inflation of People

In his 1996 book *The Great Wave*, David Hackett Fischer describes the last 1,000 years of human history as a series of price revolutions caused by demographic shifts. The basic pattern goes something like this: increases in productivity lead to social stability and higher real incomes, which encourages population growth. Population growth means more mouths to feed, which means the farming of marginal land to produce more food. Farming on lower-quality land reduces productivity, which leads to rising prices for food (inflation). Rising food prices leads to chaos and instability which in turn leads to falling populations until a new equilibrium is found. And the cycle continues. A growing agrarian labor force leads to falling real wages, lower standards of living, unrest, substance abuse, illegitimate births and a general breakdown of society. In this environment, medieval landlords were the only people to do well, as they benefited from rising rents on their land. This leads to greater social inequality, which usually results in political instability and a reduction in the birthrate. As population falls and marginal land is no longer used, productivity goes up, crop prices fall, real incomes go up, and returns on capital go down. This increases the wealth of the labor force but causes financial strain for landlords, resulting in greater equality between social classes.

So, in the pre-industrial world, life got much worse for the common man during inflationary times and actually quite a bit better during deflationary times. Meanwhile, the exact opposite was true for the landlords, or the rich. The propertied class did well during inflationary times and fell under severe financial distress during deflationary times. So, by this logic, we should welcome deflation, right? After all, if only a small minority of the ultra-affluent suffer, what's the big deal?

The problem with this argument is that today we all have a lot more in common with the medieval landlord than with the medieval peasant. In the modern, mass-affluent economy, virtually *all* of us have the trappings of the rich. We have mortgages to pay and assets to protect. We no longer live in the world of subsistence in which the affordability of food is the most pressing concern for most of humanity.

This brings us to the work of another economic historian, Gregory Clark, author of *A Farewell to Alms*. Clark explains at length the dynamics of the "Malthusian" economy, named after Thomas Malthus, the English demographer and thinker who predicted that mankind would face mass starvation by the middle of the 19th century. In the Malthusian world of scarcity, mankind survived at an equilibrium just slightly above the subsistence level. Any increase in productivity would result in higher incomes, which would result in higher birthrates. The increased number of people would push income back to the subsistence level. If, due to a famine, war, crop failure, etc., income fell below the subsistence level, people would have fewer children and would suffer higher mortality rates. The weakest among us would be the first to die until our populations thinned out enough to make subsistence living possible again. In this Darwinian world of "survival of the fittest," disease, pestilence, death and destruction were perversely the best friends of the healthy among us. If a bout of plague hit a given region and wiped out 30% of the population, all of the survivors saw their respective pieces of the income pie get 30% larger. Fewer mouths to feed meant more food for the rest of us!

Luckily, the Industrial Revolution pulled us out of this morbid cycle. For the first time in human history, ordinary people had the ability to generate real wealth and live in a society of abundance, not scarcity. In the industrial world, rising populations meant more production, better division of labor, more specialization, and higher standards of living. In the mass-affluent society that emerged, larger populations meant more consumers, more people to buy what you have to sell. The family, in the words of Brink Lindsey is his insightful book *The Age of Abundance*, became for the first time a unit of *consumption* rather than a unit of *production*.

Both Fischer and Clark take a view of inflation consistent with Keynes and the classical economists. Prices rise and fall as supply and demand shift. Like Keynes, these men focus mostly on the "demand side" of the equation, supply being limited to the arable land available to grow food. "Supply side" economics is meaningless in a pre-industrial agrarian world of low productivity growth. And Milton Friedman's contention that inflation is *always* a monetary phenomenon is simply not true. Yes, the governments of the pre-industrial era debased their currency by diluting the gold and silver content of their coins. This has been a recurring theme since the first kings issued the first coins. But this pre-industrial monetarism is clearly less significant than the demographic forces at work.

## Inflation in the Era of Mass Affluence

Fischer and Clark's work is excellent at explaining why farm prices rose and fell centuries ago. But what about today, in the modern era?

In the early 1990s, Harry S. Dent, Jr. took the inflation/deflation demographic debate in an entirely new direction. Dent argued that in a developed, service-based economy such as the United States today, labor is by far the biggest and most significant "input" in the production process. In order for employees to be viable, they must produce more in output than they cost in wages. Unfortunately, new workers produce very little in their first few months or years, yet they still have to be paid. They also need a desk and a computer or machine tools and a hard hat, not to mention office or factory space and possibly even a company car or mobile phone. And I haven't even mentioned fringe benefits such as health insurance (which I cover in the next chapter) and continuing education classes that add to the cost of each employee.

This means that when a new employee is hired, the company's expenses instantly rise but with little or no change in production. When this happens on a large scale, we have inflation. And of course, inflation doesn't start at employment. Raising and educating young people requires a massive investment from both their parents and the government. Hence, young people are inflationary from birth (or even sooner, given the rising cost of pre-natal care) until they enter the workforce and start to produce more than they cost (typically two to three years after entry). We can even take this one step further: when a career woman becomes a mother and takes maternity leave, she is temporarily removed from her normal productive capacities at work. This means that the company continues to have expenses while getting no production. Not to mention the lost productivity of mothers and fathers alike from the sleepless nights of attending to a crying baby or a sick toddler. My son Josh may be years past that stage, but I remember those nights like they were yesterday. I could continue this train of thought almost indefinitely, but you get my point: children are inflationary from birth until early career.

Of course, this is not a bad thing. Children are a necessary investment in the future. New workers eventually become highly productive, and their human capital becomes an asset to the company that hires them and to the country as a whole. Perhaps more importantly, fresh talent brings new ideas and innovations. Oftentimes, the full benefits of these innovations are not realized for decades. Consider personal computers. The key innovations in this product were made by Steve Jobs and Bill Gates by their respective companies in the early 1980s, but the resulting revolution in productivity did not happen until the mid-1990s. Companies and individuals invested millions (if not billions) of dollars before they began to truly realize a payoff.

In this context, inflation can be thought of as a means of financing new generations and the new technologies that they bring. Innovation and inflation go hand in hand.

Unfortunately for us, labor force growth actually goes negative in 2010 as Boomer retirements outnumber workforce entry by their children, the Echo Boomers. This implies that even in the absence of the debt deleveraging issues I described in Chapter 2, inflation would have ground to a halt. Naturally, this is not an exact measure. Baby Boomers could choose to work longer, which could postpone the workforce shrinkage. In the wake of the 2008 collapse, which wrecked the portfolios of many Boomers, this is exactly what we are seeing today. There could also be a shift in the percentage of women who choose to pursue gainful employment, which could shift the chart in either direction. Regardless, these changes would be marginal and the trend would remain the same. The main factor driving the deflationary forces in the years ahead is the retirement of the Boomers and a decrease in the workforce entry of their children. Fewer young professionals mean less inflation.

## But Isn't a Shrinking Workforce *In*flationary?

The common view in academia is the demographic changes facing the country are inflationary. This view, explained most eloquently by Dr. Jeremy Siegel and Federal Reserve Chairman Ben Bernanke, can be summarized like this:

As the Baby Boomers begin to retire, we will have comparatively fewer workers. This means that a smaller number of workers will have to work to support the consumption needs of the country. Fewer workers mean less production, or supply. If supply falls while demand remains the same, prices will have to rise as the marketplace reacts. Thus, we will have inflation. Furthermore, a shortage of labor could develop, which would force companies to raise wages in order to compete for workers, adding further inflationary pressure. The end result will be a form of 1970s-style stagflation, so the thinking goes.

While this view has its intuitive appeal, there are several flaws. I will debunk these flaws by using the example of a single extended family.

When a man and woman marry or begin to live together, they have certain economies of scale. Renting one apartment or making one mortgage payment is cheaper than two. Likewise, the couple shares one set of utility bills, furniture, linens, kitchen utensils and every other facet of modern life.

When the couple begins to have children, life gets a lot more expensive. Suddenly, that small apartment needs to be bigger, as does the car. In addition to their regular expenses, the new parents can also add Junior's baby food, clothes, medical bills and day care to the list. Things only get worse as Junior ages. Soon, the parents find themselves paying for swimming lessons, band camp and college prep classes.

At this stage in his life, Junior is an inflationary pressure on the household. He produces nothing of economic value yet he consumes more and more, as all youngsters do—on Mom and Dad's tab. Luckily for Mom and Dad's finances, Junior eventually moves out and gets a job. About this time, however, Grandma retires and decides to move into Junior's old room at Mom and Dad's house.

In the Siegel/Bernanke model, Grandma is considered to be every bit as inflationary as Junior, which assumes that children and the retired are interchangeable parts. Both consume and neither produce. Therefore, both are inflationary, right?

Not so fast! Empirical evidence (and common sense) would tell us that a person's consumer spending is highly dependent on that person's age and stage of life, as I covered in Chapter 5. People today can be expected to spend more every year of their life until their late 40s or early 50s. With retirement in sight, people begin to consume less and save more. With the exception of health care, spending on virtually everything decreases in late career and retirement. Sure, Grandma has to eat, but she doesn't eat as much as a growing Junior, and Grandma isn't buying a new closet of clothes every six months, a basketball hoop or the latest iPod. And she certainly isn't buying a new washer or dryer, a big-screen plasma TV or driving 20,000 miles per year as a taxi service for a child. It is the purchase of these big-ticket durable goods that boosts aggregate demand, and consumers peak in their demand for these items much earlier than retirement. This is the fundamental flaw in the Siegel/Bernanke argument. An aging population full of retirees spends substantially less money (especially on the highly leveraged durable goods) and is *de*flationary, not *in*flationary.

Siegel and Bernanke's view is contrary to the logic of the economic historians mentioned above—Fischer, Clark and Dent—and to the recent real-life experience of Japan. All of the research described above makes a compelling point that falling (or aging) populations are deflationary. Yet the inflationary view persists and appears to be gaining acceptance. So there you have it. In this chapter, I brought out the academic "big guns" to drive home a couple very important points. First of all, inflation is *not* controlled by the Fed. The Fed is an important contributor, of course. But demographics are the real force to be reckoned with. And demographic trends support the view that deflation will be more of a threat than inflation. Any inflation in the years ahead should be mild, provided of course that the Fed doesn't spend enough to turn us into a banana republic.

There is one *enormous* exception to this, however. As I mentioned in the example of the extended family, we tend to spend a lot more money on health care as we age. So, even in a period of negligible overall consumer price inflation, demographic forces could cause significant inflation in certain subsectors of the economy, and perhaps none more than health care, so let's talk about it next.

# Chapter 9:

# Health Care, Insurance and Taxes

Taxes are always one of the biggest points of contention no matter where you live. However, if like myself you happen to live and work in the high-tax state of California, then it takes on a whole new meaning. Every dollar we spend in taxes is a dollar we cannot spend on ourselves, so we expect our government to spend those dollars wisely.

With this in mind, I am reminded of a very insightful quote from Leon Levy, a legendary investor and one of the founders of the Oppenheimer family of mutual funds: **"Tax codes reflect the values of a society."**

When Levy wrote this in his book *The Mind of Wall Street* he used the word "reflect," but what he should have said is "shape." Rightly or wrongly, there are few methods of persuasion (or coercion) as effective as the tax code. As Levy continues,

> It is no accident that the French produce great wine. The French tax code used to favor the producers of the spectacular first-growth wines, who were taxed at a lower rate than those who made *vin ordinaire*. The tax code thus gave producers an incentive to improve their wines. I have thought about the myriad ways in which money flows toward tax incentives and away from high taxes and have concluded that **taxes play a profound role in shaping history**. Give officials control of the tax code and they can change society, either deliberately through the wise use of incentives or, more commonly, inadvertently through a misunderstanding of how people react to taxes.[20]

Well said, Mr. Levy. Think about this for a minute. In how many ways has tax policy shifted the behavior of companies and individuals in the United States?

An obvious example is the mortgage interest deduction, which made owning a home more affordable but which also encouraged Americans to buy bigger and more expensive homes than they otherwise might have. It also nudged marginal homebuyers of questionable credit quality into buying homes using subprime mortgages—and we *know* how that turned out. The tax deduction was "successful" in that it accomplished the government goal of increasing home ownership. Of course, it's a matter of debate as to whether this was a worthwhile policy, particularly after the mortgage meltdown of 2007-2009.

The government has somewhat mixed motives when it comes to taxing vices. In the late 1910s, one of the biggest arguments against national prohibition of alcohol was not personal freedom; it was the loss of tax revenue for the Federal government. The progressives who campaigned for 18th amendment—which gave us prohibition—first had to campaign for the 16th amendment—which gave us the income tax and the IRS. Naturally, during the pits of the Great Depression, when income tax receipts were plummeting, President Roosevelt abandoned his previous "dry" views and became a proponent of legalizing alcohol again.

Similarly, while the state governments publically have to condemn the tobacco companies, they would be devastated if Americans actually quit smoking. The loss of tax revenue would be a disaster, especially during this period of falling income and property tax receipts. So, they continue their little song and dance—continuing to tax and regulate the industry while making sure that they don't kill the goose that lays all of those golden eggs.

In a sign of true desperation during the crisis in 2008, the governor of New York proposed a punishing tax on fattening food and drink. As Clyde Haberman described it in the *New York Times*,

> With his tax proposals this week, Gov. David A. Paterson joined a long line of New York leaders who have counted on self-wounding, even self-destructive behavior to help them dig out of budget holes. **Mr. Paterson called for a huge tax,**

**18 percent, on sugary sodas and juice drinks.** It's a public health measure, his lieutenants said—you know, to counter the obesity epidemic.

Sure. The $404 million tax haul that the governor expects next year is merely incidental, right?[21]

If Mr. Haberman has a touch of cynicism in his writing, he is certainly entitled to it. New Yorkers have seen this before, always with the stated intent of preserving public health. But, as Mr. Haberman continues, "The last thing that government wants is for everyone, right this minute, to stop smoking, boozing, gambling and downing those nutritionally empty supersweet sodas. Too much money is at stake."

As if the fat tax was not bad enough, the governor also proposed 88 assorted sales or use tax hikes, most notably on clothes, taxis, movie tickets, and "digitally delivered entertainment services" such as iTunes. Of course, these hikes probably will have unintended consequences, such as a transfer of business to out-of-state "e-tailers" like Amazon. com that are not subject to sales taxes. This will hurt New York's store owners. The hikes also are likely to lead to increased smuggling and, in the case of the iTunes tax, even greater levels of Internet piracy.

In the business world, consider the case of corporate dividends. There is a considerable amount of academic literature discussing the "principle-agent" problem of corporate management. Managers do not always act in the best interests of shareholders; they often have their own agendas, driven perhaps by ego and the desire to "build empires" (and ultimately, to secure large paychecks for themselves.) The result is that they often waste a large amount of investor capital on suboptimal projects.

The dividend is an excellent tool to keep managements in line. Paying out cold, hard cash to investors limits managers' ability to use aggressive accounting to make themselves look better; they must have the actual cash to back it up. Plus, by taking excess cash out of the hands of ambitious CEOs, you force them to do more with less, encouraging efficiency and better use of investor capital.

So, if dividends are so great, why do most companies pay out such a small percentage of their earnings? As you might guess, the answer is taxes. The double taxation of dividends makes it woefully tax-inefficient to pay investors in cash. So instead, companies often use their earnings to make "investments" of questionable value or in buying back their own shares. In theory, share buybacks are equivalent to dividends in delivering shareholder value; in practice, managements tend to be horrible market timers, buying their own shares when prices are expensive at bull market tops and failing to buy when stocks are cheap at bear market bottoms—yet another way for them to burn investor capital.

## Death and Taxes

Perhaps no tax is more controversial than the "death tax." The estate tax has a long and colorful history and is actually one of the oldest taxes in America; it has been used at varying times and in varying forms since colonial times. In the Old World, its use can be traced all the way to the Egyptian pharaohs in 700 BC. Likewise, Caesar Augustus imposed an estate tax in ancient Rome (which is ironic, because Augustus himself rose to power with the inheritance he received from the slain Julius Caesar, in what could be the most famous contested probate case in history). The Heritage Foundation published a brief history of the estate tax in its January 2004 issue of the *Backgrounder*.22 I will summarize their history in the paragraphs below.

The first U.S. experiment with an estate tax was the 1797 Stamp Act, used to pay off debts from the undeclared war with France. The act required a federal stamp on all wills in probate. It was repealed in 1804, and Americans were spared the estate tax until the Civil War, when the Tax Act of 1862 used an inheritance tax to raise funds for the federal army. Lincoln's inheritance tax was repealed in 1870 after the dust had settled, and Americans were again spared the estate tax until the next major war.

World War I and the ensuing reduction in world trade cut into the United States' tariff revenues, leading to the passage of the 16th Amendment and the creation of the IRS. The estate tax was brought back yet again and was dramatically increased the following year when the United States entered the war. Alas, it has been with us ever since.

Once the funding needs for the war subsided, policy makers reinvented the estate tax as a form of income redistribution. This was largely popular in a country where wealth was concentrated in the hands of a few well-known families—with names like Rockefeller, Morgan and Ford. However, in the following decades, as the United States progressed into a mass-affluent society, millions of Americans who would at most have considered themselves to be upper middle class have found themselves subject to a rather unpleasant surprise upon the death of a loved one.

Estate tax reform began in the late 1970s, but the reform did not come close to keeping pace with the rise in American wealth. Americans of comparatively average means continued to find themselves subject to the estate tax until former President Bush's tax reforms began to address this.

Just *Dying* to Save on the Estate Tax

Economics is a study of events at the margin, and Kopczuk and Slemrod's 2001 paper, "Dying to Save Taxes: Evidence from Estate Tax Returns on the Death Elasticity," is a fascinating look at how timing decisions are affected by tax policy.

Kopczuk and Slemrod write:

> There is also evidence that financial considerations affect the timing of decisions that are not generally thought of as being "economic." For example, Sjoquist and Walker (1995) conclude from an analysis of Census data that the marriage penalty embedded in the U.S. income tax has a significant negative effect on the timing of marriages: as the penalty increases, fewer couples marry in the months of November and December relative to the number of marriages during the first few months of spring in the new year....
>
> [Likewise], Dickert-Conlin and Chandra (1999) find that the timing of births is sensitive to tax incentives. Under the U.S. tax system, the tax benefits of having a child are (fully) realized only if the birth takes place before midnight, January 1. Using a sample of children from the National Longitudinal Survey of Youth, Dickert-Conlin and Chandra find that the probability that a child is born in the last week of December, rather than the first week of January, is positively correlated with tax benefits from so doing; they estimate that increasing the tax benefit by $500 raises the probability of having a child in the last week of December by 26.9 percent.

Surprisingly, a mere $500 tax break encourages a surge of births in the last week of the year. The authors later admit that they cannot say whether this phenomenon is due to natural causes, doctor-induced labor, or even ex post facto falsification of the birth records to get the tax benefit. Kopczuk and Slemrod continue:

If birth, why not death?...There is a substantial body of evidence corroborating this phenomenon in other contexts. Phillips and King (1988) report that, among Jews, the number of deaths was lower than expected in the week before Passover and higher than expected in the week after; the pattern was most pronounced in years when the holiday fell on a weekend, when it is most likely to be celebrated by the largest number of people. Phillips and Smith (1990) find that mortality among Chinese dips by 35.1% in the week before the Harvest Moon festival and peaks by the same amount in the week after. Anson and Anson (1997) find a similar effect related to the timing of Ramadan for Moslems living in Israel, and note that the effect was larger for women than for men, reflecting their different roles in the celebration of the holy day rites.

Kopczuk and Slemrod go on to say that "...a non-zero death elasticity is consistent with the notion of a bequest motive." In other words, if the timing of death is somewhat flexible, people will subtly alter the timing of their death to avoid the estate tax and thus to pass on more money to their heirs. Putting some numbers behind this, the authors found that, among those dying within two weeks before or after a change in the estate tax rate, a $10,000 potential tax savings increases the probability of dying before the tax hike by 1.6%. Of course, whether this was altruism on the part of the dying is up for debate.

The authors point out that some decisions, such as whether to remain on life support or to "pull the plug" are made not by the dying person but by their heirs. Thus, it is not clear whether the authors' findings were indicative of altruism on the part of the dying or cold manipulation on the part of would-be beneficiaries. At any rate, the data makes it obvious that tax policy does indeed have a predictable effect on human behavior, be it an altruistic or calloused one. Just a little something for our lawmakers to keep in mind as they prepare to negotiate the future direction of the estate tax!

One of the hallmarks of George W. Bush's fiscal program was the elimination of the estate tax and a reduction in taxes in general. President Obama has indicated that he intends to bring back the estate tax when its repeal automatically expires after 2010, although he would like to keep the exempted amount at the 2009 level of $3.5 million. The tax rate applied to estates above that threshold would be 45%.

No legislation has been passed as of this writing, and Congress may have other ideas. Ultimately, tax laws are crafted by Congress, not the president. Bottom line: Even if your net worth currently exempts you for the estate tax, understand that these levels and rates can be changed at the pleasure of Congress at any time. Hope for the best, but prepare for the worst.

The Health Care Crisis and the Tax Code

Many Americans fear that we are heading towards a government-controlled, socialized medical system. But what few seem to realize is that we are essentially already there, at least by some measures.

The governments of Canada and the United Kingdom—the two countries most often referenced as having "socialized medicine"—spend 7.0% and 7.3% of their respective GDPs on health care. The United States, via Medicare, Medicaid, and other smaller programs, also spends 7% of GDP—and a much larger GDP at that (Figure 9.1).

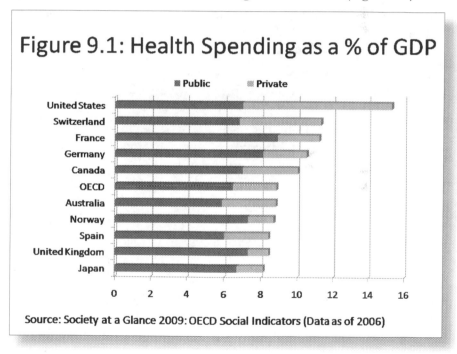

Figure 9.1: Health Spending as a % of GDP

Source: Society at a Glance 2009: OECD Social Indicators (Data as of 2006)

Private spending, paid by patients and insurance companies, more than doubles the U.S. total with an additional 8.3%. Combining public and private health spending, health care in the United States is vastly more expensive than anywhere else in the world. And as both statistical measures and casual observation attest, the average American is not any healthier than the average European or Japanese citizen. On the high-end, America is still the world leader in cutting-edge medical techniques. But this does not explain why the prices of basic, standard medical procedures are more expensive here than in other developed nations. It is almost mind-boggling that Japan—despite its enormous population of elderly citizens—spends barely half what the United States does relative to GDP.

With this in mind, let us now consider the state of health care in America. I think we all agree that the system is broken and something has to be done. The Obama health plan was an ambitious attempt at reform, but as it stands it is clearly unrealistic, intrusive and unaffordable given the current budget deficit and national debt. But in defending the status quo, the Republicans are also wrong. The system as it currently stands is absolutely indefensible. There is no justifiable reason for our health system to be roughly twice as expensive as Canada's and the UK's while simultaneously leaving a large minority of the country uninsured. It's fair to ask: What exactly are we getting for our money?

Rather than simply protest the Obama plan and threaten to de-fund it, the Republicans should make themselves useful by promoting *real* reform. President Bush, for his many perceived faults, managed to find a good idea with Health Savings Accounts (HSAs) coupled with high-deductible insurance policies. The former president also proposed making employer-provided insurance "taxable" (though with an offsetting tax credit) in order to make Americans better realize the true cash value of the benefits that they have come to view as "free."

HSAs and tax accounting gimmicks are by no means a comprehensive solution, but they were a step in the right direction. If the Republicans really want to make a positive impact on the country's long term health (and fiscal health too, for that matter), they will show Americans that their only two choices are not a dysfunctional status quo and an ObamaCare "solution" that will bankrupt the country. They need to propose better alternatives.

As you might have guessed, the tax code is a major contributing factor to the spiraling cost of health care. In my view, the two biggest problems are the "fee for service" compensation model for doctors, which encourages unnecessary testing and procedures, and the high price of malpractice insurance. (These two actually contribute to one another.) The tax code, with its perverse incentives, comes in third.

Essentially, doctors do not get paid for results. They get paid for individual "a la carte" procedures. So, they have every *dis*incentive to attack medical problems in an efficient, holistic way. I do not fault the doctors for this. They didn't create this monster. They, like the rest of us, are just trying to survive the best they can, and in any event doctors do not receive much of the money in question. Take a look at Figure 9.2. Much of the money gets lost in the black hole of administration. *The percentage of health spending that actually goes to the doctor is a miniscule 22%.*

The problem is that nearly all insurance companies take their pricing model from Medicare guidelines, which encourages the "fee-for-service" model. If Medicare and the broader insurance industry is to remain viable with the aging of the Baby Boomers on the horizon, this must be scrapped. Doctors must be properly incentivized to "fix" medical problems in a more efficient manner. And the reform, if it is to be successful, must start with Medicare.

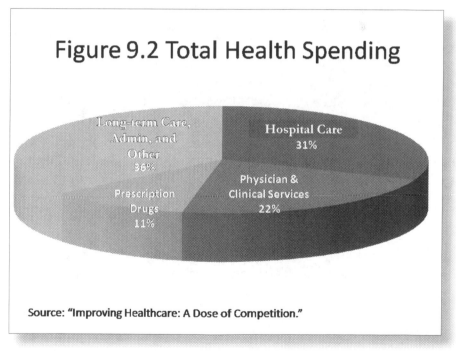

# Figure 9.2 Total Health Spending

Long-term Care, Admin, and Other 36%

Hospital Care 31%

Prescription Drugs 11%

Physician & Clinical Services 22%

Source: "Improving Healthcare: A Dose of Competition."

The second issue, tort reform to reduce the cost of malpractice insurance, ties in very closely with the first. Most Americans would agree that the tort system is out of control. How many of us have watched with disgust (and probably a little envy) as one of our countrymen gets a huge legal settlement far out of proportion to the damage received. Remember the woman who sued McDonalds for millions—and won— after burning herself with hot coffee?

Doctors, fearful of being sued for malpractice, order massive amounts of unnecessary tests and procedures in order to avoid "looking" negligent and leaving themselves open to a malpractice lawsuit. And at the end of the day, the patient doesn't mind (and probably doesn't even notice), because the tab is picked up by their insurance company or the government, and thus "socialized" across the broader population. No one in this chain has any incentive to exercise restraint because, while the costs to society are high, the costs in each case to each person individually are low—generally limited to a nominal co-pay of $20 or so.

This brings us back to my original point about taxes. People and companies, though not "hyper-rational" like the beings described in economics textbooks, generally respond to monetary incentives. Let us consider employer-provided health insurance, which most Americans working for large companies enjoy.

Americans have come to view it as a given that their employer is responsible for providing health insurance while simultaneously viewing it as "socialist" for the government to provide these same services. But why is this?

During the labor shortages of World War II, companies needed to raise wages in order to attract workers, but wartime wage and price controls prevented them from doing so. Health insurance and other benefits became the solution, as they gave companies the ability to effectively increase wages while staying within the letter of the law. As the years rolled by, Congress began to view this arrangement as a social good and created tax incentives to encourage it. Today, your company can write off the value of benefits provided to you, but you do not have to pay income taxes on these benefits. This makes health insurance an extremely tax-efficient way to compensate employees. Unfortunately, it also makes absolutely no economic sense.

Americans view state-provided health insurance as "socialism," but fail to view tax-subsidized insurance using the employer as an intermediary in the same light. Those who defend our "free market" health system are simply wrong. Our system is not "free market" at all, but corporatist. Like the Europeans and Canadians, we too have socialized medicine, only in our system private employers act as middle men.

There are economic consequences for this, of course. American companies have to maintain expensive HR departments to administer benefits, and the insurance premiums paid are real money. This puts them at a disadvantage to foreign competitors who have no such obligation. Consider the pre-bankruptcy General Motors. General Motors could not compete with Toyota and other rivals because health benefits for current and retired workers added more than $2,000 *per car* produced. With a $2,000 cost disadvantage, it was only a matter of time until General Motors bled to death. The financial crisis sped up the process, but it would have happened on its own eventually.

So, while I am critical of the employer-provided insurance model, this is *not* to say I favor socialized medicine. Given the horrid lack of cost control in the Medicare program, I believe that socialized medicine or "socialized medicine lite" via ObamaCare would be an expensive mistake. **President Obama's plan would simply make a bad system worse.**

Costs can be lowered with the proper incentives—and the tax code can play a significant role in this endeavor. Health costs can be reduced in this country with a reevaluation of the fee-for-service model (starting with Medicare), medical tort reform and an expansion of the consumer-directed health care model, which includes such products as HSAs. But on a more fundamental level, Americans must first come to realize that insurance and medical care are not "free" in any system, be it free-market, corporatist or socialist. We all pay the bill one way or another.

Moral Hazard at the Doctor's Office

No, this section has nothing to do with stem cell research or doctor-assisted suicide. Moral hazard is a very real phenomenon whenever people are shielded from the consequences of their decisions.

Banking is a fine example. Before the Great Depression, there were no protections on your savings other than the good reputation of the bank holding them. A prudent saver in that era would only deposit his or her hard-earned cash in a conservative, safe institution. Unfortunately, the Depression nearly took down the entire banking system, good and bad banks alike. As a result we now have FDIC federal insurance that protects your savings in the event that your bank fails. Most economists view the development of FDIC insurance as a good thing, in that it encourages savers to take their cash out from under the mattress and put it into the system, where it can be used to finance economic growth. Of course, the very same economists would add the caveat that this insurance also has the effect of encouraging excessive risk taking and general carelessness by depositors. After all, why bother investigating the bank's solvency if the government is the one shouldering the risk?

"But," you might protest, "there are costs to the taxpayer. We all pay more in taxes after a federal bailout of a failed bank."

Yes, this is true. ***But the incremental cost to each individual is small relative to the cost to the system as a whole.*** No single person has an incentive to act responsibly. This is moral hazard in action. And believe it or not, the situation is even worse when it comes to health care for a number of reasons. First, health care, rightly or wrongly, has a sense of entitlement that other expenses simply do not have. People believe that they have a right to health care, or at the very least, a right to "not die." Not surprisingly, this idea that cost is irrelevant when it comes to saving or improving lives leads to higher costs. After all, it is fine to talk about cutting medical costs, but when it is *your* family member in the emergency room, those concerns naturally get thrown to the wind. Adding to this is the fact that Medicare is the ultimate payer in many cases, and most people (rightly or wrongly) seem to have no moral qualms with soaking the government. Most patients probably don't even realize that they're doing it.

For perhaps the best analogy to the moral hazard issue, consider Richard Epstein's analogy of teenagers sharing a soda:

> Think of two ways in which a group of 10 teenagers can drink soda at a luncheon counter. One is to get a large pitcher and have 10 thirsty kids each use a straw to take out what he or she wants. The second is to divide the soda into glasses, and assign them one to a person. Let there be 10 pints and each teenager's initial entitlement is one pint either way. The patterns of consumption of the soda will not be the same in these two arrangements. Even if by some miracle each person gets the same amount of soda in the two configurations (which they won't), **we can be 100 percent confident that the soda will be more rapidly consumed when all 10 teenagers slurp their soft drink from the common pitcher**. Consumption rates will slow markedly if each has his or her own glass, for slow sipping now results in greater satisfaction, not a reduction in individual share.[23]

Again, one of the major problems is that the pricing of medical care in this country is either directly or indirectly dictated by Medicare, and Medicare uses an administrative formula which calculates "appropriate" prices based upon imperfect estimates and fudge factors. Rather than independently calculate prices, private insurers in this country almost universally use Medicare prices as a framework to negotiate payments.[24]

This adds an entirely new element to the moral hazard that plagues the industry. Not only do patients push all responsibility for controlling costs into the hands of insurance companies, but the companies themselves push all of the responsibility into the hands of Medicare! If an insurance company is overcharged for a routine procedure, they can simply raise premiums on the patient's insurance plan and then blame the Medicare pricing scheme for the whole debacle. In the case of company-sponsored plans, an additional level of unaccountability is added since the premiums are paid by the company, not the user of the insurance. Since none of the participants in this little game has any incentive to exercise discipline, it's no shock that excessive and unjustified costs consume as much as 20% of health care spending.[25] With no real responsibility at any point in the chain, it's shocking that our system isn't even more dysfunctional that it is.

One of the best explanations of moral hazard was Mark Pauly's 1968 paper published in the *American Economic Review*.[26] One point that Mr. Pauly emphasizes is that health insurance offers incentives for patients to *over-consume* health care. True insurance is designed to protect the policyholder from random, unpredictable and catastrophic events, such as his house being struck by lightning. Insurance is *not* designed to pay for routine house painting and maintenance. Yet somehow, these same principals have been lost in health insurance. We don't buy health insurance just to protect ourselves from catastrophic diseases, like cancer. We also use it for yearly flu shots and amoxicillin, the medical equivalents of painting and routine maintenance. In practice, it appears that we do not view health insurance as insurance at all, but rather as a medical pre-paid card. More accurately, it could be described as a gift certificate in that we end up buying things that we would never normally buy if we were using our *own* money. The result is that we over-consume on expenditures that are often frivolous and drive the price higher than it needs to be.

Pauly writes:

> [In order for health insurance to be optimal], the costs of medical care must be random variables. But if such expenses are not completely random, the proposition no longer holds. The quantity of medical care an individual will demand depends on his income and tastes, how ill he is, and the price charged for

> it. ***The effect of an insurance which indemnifies against all medical care expenses is to reduce the price charged to the individual at the point of service from the market price to zero.***

Whether or not insurance encourages over-consumption depends on the **elasticity of demand** for health care. In other words, the elasticity of demand refers to how flexible your purchase decision is. Your demand for food is inflexible—you need it to live. But your demand for, say, beef is very flexible. If it gets too expensive, you can buy chicken instead.

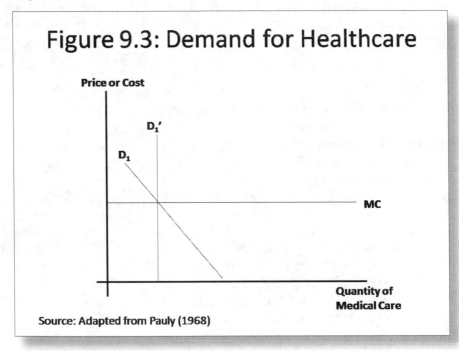

# Figure 9.3: Demand for Healthcare

Source: Adapted from Pauly (1968)

Figure 9.3 illustrates this graphically. Line $D_1'$ is an example of inelastic demand, and as you can see, the amount of health care demanded is the same at all price levels. This is pretty close to reality for life-saving procedures, such as an emergency heart bypass surgery. However, most medical decisions look a lot more like $D_1$. The amount of care demanded decreases as the price increases. There are quite a few noncritical medical procedures you might be willing to forgo were the price high enough. They might be highly desirable, but at some price they are just not worth it. This is where over-consumption and moral hazard comes into play.

As Pauly continues: "Each individual may well recognize that 'excess' use of medical care makes the premium he must pay rise. No individual will be motivated to restrain his own use, however, since the incremental benefit to him for excess use is great, while the additional cost of his use is largely spread over other insurance holders, and so he bears only a tiny fraction of the cost of his use."

This is Epstein's analogy of the teenagers and the pitcher of soda in action. The teenagers end up drinking more soda and drinking it faster with little if any effect on their portion of the lunch tab.

So what's the solution? Abolish all forms of insurance? Doing so would eliminate moral hazard and almost definitely lower prices, but is that really what we want? Most people would lack the financial means to pay for major surgeries and life-saving treatments when they became necessary. Clearly, some kind of insurance is needed. Pauly suggests restricting insurance to cover only catastrophic and relatively random illnesses, like cancer or heart disease. This would be consistent with products such as Health Savings Accounts ("HSAs"), which combine a high-deductible insurance policy with a tax-advantaged savings account. Since it is the *patient's* money and not the insurance company's at stake, patients and doctors alike are likely to use a little more discipline. The result should be lower medical bills, lower premiums, and fewer over-worked doctors.

While any form of insurance is bound to introduce moral hazard into the system, this is not entirely bad. As Clark Havighurst explains, "A degree of moral hazard is a natural concomitant of any arrangement, private or public, that gives people security about their future health care costs. Because such financial security is valuable to people, it is not irrational to incur some higher costs to obtain it."[27] Well said, and I agree completely. We all want security when it comes to our health. The key will be to keep the costs of moral hazard in the health industry to a tolerable minimum, especially given the demands that our system will face as the Boomers age and require ever-increasing amounts of care. For any system to be viable with a looming burden as large as the one we face, there must be a mechanism to make consumers more financially accountable for the services they use. Unfortunately, this means that higher out-of-pocket health care costs for consumers are virtually guaranteed.

This chapter has come a very long way for me to make my original point: even in a period of stable or slightly falling consumer prices, there can be significant inflation in certain parts of the economy. Health care, unfortunately, is one of them. Some kind of reform—*real* reform—will eventually happen because it has to. There are practical limits to how much Americans can pay for health care.

Unfortunately, the necessary reforms may still be several years away. America, like most democratic countries, tends to put off difficult decisions until the absolute last moment. It's just one of those quirks of democracy. No matter how idealistic he might be, a politician's primary objective is always to get reelected. For this reason, big reforms are usually only possible when a crisis reaches a boiling point and voters demand them. We're not quite there—*yet*.

Bottom line: Change will come, eventually. But for the next several years, plan on rising medical prices being the reality. If you currently get your insurance from your employer, expect them to push more of that cost to you.

# Chapter 10:

# The Art of Managing Risk

One of the key lessons in finance is that there is no such thing as a free lunch. If it sounds too good to be true, it probably is.

In the world of investments, we pay for our returns by the risk we take in order to get them. In a bull market, this seems like a pretty good trade-off. Investors made a killing in stocks in the 1990s and a *leveraged* killing on their homes in the 2000s. Unfortunately, the bill came due in the form of the bear market of 2000-2002 and the housing crash and financial meltdown of 2007 to the present. Suddenly, investors realized how costly those earlier returns had been, and it seemed like a pretty rotten deal!

Investment risk takes a couple different forms. The most benign— but still quite serious—is opportunity cost. This can be thought of as the returns you *didn't* earn because you invested in something else. For example, if you earned 5% in a bond fund, but the stock fund you didn't buy returned 12%, your opportunity cost is the difference between the two, or 7%.

No one has a crystal ball, of course, and we all suffer from opportunity cost at one time or another. Even the great Warren Buffett, the most successful investor in history, misses out on countless opportunities every year. It's just a part of life that comes from not having perfect foresight. We're only human, after all.

As investors, we can minimize our opportunity cost by assessing the amount of risk we are prepared to take and allocating our capital to the investments that, given the imperfect information we have to work with, offer the best potential return for the level of risk we're taking.

But more fundamentally—and this goes to the heart of the practice of any wealth advisor or investor—it is best not to fixate on opportunity cost and instead keep the goal in mind. Rather than chase the highest return possible—and put my clients on a financial roller coaster ride that they neither need nor want—I find it makes far more sense to start with the goal and work backwards. If a client starts with $2,000,000 and needs $6,000,000 in the next 15 years to meet his retirement and legacy goals, we can figure out what return is needed to meet that goal and invest accordingly, taking the least amount of risk possible to achieve the necessary return.

The risk that keeps many in this business awake at night is the risk of outright loss. There are different ways to define this risk. In the investment management industry, it is standard practice to define risk as volatility. This is the basis of modern portfolio theory, which was developed in the 1950s by Harry Markowitz. In the Markowitz model, risk is the degree to which a given investment fluctuates in value. For the math geeks in the room, this is numerically calculated as the "standard deviation of returns." In the decades that followed Markowitz's breakthrough, this concept has been adapted slightly. Some readers might have heard of a stock or mutual fund's "beta." Beta is the degree to which an investment fluctuates *relative* to its benchmark (usually the S&P 500). An investment with a beta of 1.0 is expected to fluctuate in line with the market. A beta of 1.5 would imply that the investment was 50% more volatile, and a beta of 0.5 would imply that it is half as volatile.

While mathematically elegant, this is not how most people think in the real word. This kind of thinking is also shunned by many "old school" value investors who follow in the footsteps of Benjamin Graham and Warren Buffett. Graham, the father of the investment management profession, considered risk to be the permanent impairment of capital. In other words, risk is the possibility that your investments fall in value and never recover. Investors in General Motors, Bear Stearns, Lehman Brothers, or any of the other companies that went bankrupt during the meltdown would understand this risk all too well.

In this chapter, I want to discuss some of the issues surrounding the popular measures for risk. The goal here is to make a case for a more holistic approach to risk—one that will save your nest egg from the next major financial debacle, whenever it might strike.

When Genius Failed

As Roger Lowenstein recounts in his classic *When Genius Failed*, the financial world came very close to ending in 1998, even during one of the strongest bull markets in history. Earlier in the decade, some of the brightest minds in finance—the guys that literally wrote the books that Ivy League finance students study in college—started a hedge fund with the rather boring name of Long Term Capital Management (LTCM).[28] The group included noted Nobel-Prize-winning scholars such as Myron Scholes (the co-creator of the Black-Scholes option pricing formula) and Robert Merton and Wall Street legends like John Meriwether of Salomon Brothers fame.

The professors and their Wall Street partners sought to take advantage of what they thought were irrational discrepancies in the pricing of similar investments. For example, if French bonds appeared to be cheap relative to German bonds based on their historical relationship, you would buy French bonds and sell German bonds, making money as French bonds rose relative to the German bonds. Of course, the risk involved was that the irrational pricing could go the other way and widen even further, creating a loss. In other words, the market could go from irrational to *more* irrational.

The professors were not making these trades haphazardly. They used the same financial tools that the industry continues to use today. According to these "normal" tools, the risk of Long-Term Capital Management taking a 10% loss was about 1 in 1,000 years.[29] The risk of a 50% loss was approximately 1 in 10,000,000,000,000,000,000,000,00 0,000,000,000 years, or several billion times the age of our universe. (An event of this magnitude is known as a *Black Swan*.) Suffice it to say, based on the tools used to measure risk, the fund appeared about as close to "riskless" as you can get.

As you might have already guessed, that's not quite how things worked out in the real world. That "once in a billion years" event happened after just five years. The problem was that the professors' risk models were based on poor assumptions that do *not* hold up in the real world—the very same assumptions that are used today by many in the investment industry and individual investors.

First, they assumed that the distribution of returns for investments or portfolios was "normal," meaning that they followed a bell curve.

Second, they expected investments to behave in the future in the same way they had behaved in the recent past .

Nassim Nicholas Taleb, author of the best-selling *Fooled by Randomness* and *The Black Swan* refers to this as the **"problem of induction."** In finance, we base our view of what is possible on what has already happened. Our estimates of returns and volatility are based on the past and then presented as if these "odds" are truly predictable, like a roll of the dice. We know that the odds of rolling any one number on a die are one in six. We don't know what the odds of hitting a certain return in the stock market are. The problem is that the tools used in the industry assume that we *do* know the odds, and this assumption is dangerous. It lulls investors into a false sense of security about the level of risk they are taking. Related to this is what Taleb calls the **"ludic fallacy,"** or the temptation to view the world of investing like a game of chance. The stock market is often considered to be a form of casino gambling in which one side wins and one side loses. This is certainly a fair comparison. The problem is that the stock market is actually *worse* than a casino. A casino is a closed system in which you can pre-calculate the odds and the rules do not change halfway through your hand of blackjack. Your chances of receiving an ace will not be 4/52 on one draw and 10/51 on the next. Betting limits do not arbitrarily change at the poker table. The number of red or black spaces on the roulette wheel does not change with every spin. In the real world of finance, all of these things *do* happen. The stock market is not a roll of the dice, unless you can find a pair of dice that has the ability to change shape after it leaves your hand.

Taleb has dedicated his entire career to debunking this kind of thinking using the example of the **Black Swan,**[30] which originally came from the work of the philosopher Karl Popper. Popper made the observation that you can observe a million swans that are white and draw the conclusion that *all* swans are white—but it only takes the sighting of *one* black swan to prove your theory completely wrong. Europeans believed that all swans were white because they had never observed a black one—until British sailors spotted black swans in Australia during the colonial period. Just because they hadn't seen them before didn't mean they didn't exist.

Taleb took this idea and applied it to modern investing, and I believe his thinking is worth noting. After Taleb popularized the term, "black swan" has come to mean any low probability, high impact event. By nature, they are unpredictable and it is virtually impossible to accurately calculate the odds of one occurring, but when they happen the results are catastrophic. For example, the terror attack of September 11, 2001, was a black swan. No one had ever committed a terrorist act by ramming a plane into a skyscraper before, so it never occurred to Americans to be prepared for it—much less calculate the odds of it happening. The 1987 stock market crash and the 2010 "flash crash" in which the Dow Jones Industrial Average fell almost 10% in a matter of minutes are examples of black swans specifically stemming from the market itself.

Taleb—himself a veteran quantitative trader—takes issue with the modern tendency to quantify risk as a *precise* number. Risk is no longer a concept; it's a *number*. This leads to a false sense of security as we rely on a degree of precision that simply isn't there. Think about the subprime mortgage disaster. Banks took far more risk than they should have in lending far too much money on inflated properties to borrowers who often lacked the means to pay. Why? Because their risk models told them it was ok. Similarly, how many "quant" hedge funds blew up during the crisis? The traders traded far more aggressively than would be prudent because their elaborate risk models gave them a false sense of security. Models, of course, are only as good as their inputs. You put garbage in, you get garbage out. It really doesn't matter how elegant the formulas are.

This echoes the words of John Maynard Keynes a generation ago when he said *"I'd rather be generally right than precisely wrong."* It also ties in with legendary value investor Benjamin Graham who focused on "margin of safety" in his investments and passed that wisdom on to his protégé, Warren Buffett. Buffett jokes that he likes his investments to wear both a belt *and* suspenders. Because you can never fully know the future or take all unknown risks into account, you need that all-important margin of safety, which is all too lacking in modern financial theory.

## The Unknown Unknowns

"There are known knowns. These are things we know that we know. There are known unknowns. That is to say, there are things that we know we don't know. But there are also unknown unknowns. There are things we don't know we don't know." —Donald Rumsfeld, Former U.S. Secretary of Defense

The above quote is a little convoluted, but it's a valid observation. We plan for things that we know will occur, "known knowns," such as anticipating a curve in the road while driving. Things that we know are possible but we do not know when or if they will occur, such as having a heart attack, are called "known unknowns." Naturally, we don't know when a heart attack might strike, so we buy health insurance to mitigate our risk.

It is the final category, "unknown unknowns," that make life complicated. These are risks that we haven't even imagined.

The September 11 attacks were an example of an unknown unknown, in that no one predicted terrorists would be able to use a hijacked plane, much less several of them, as a missile to take down a building. This is probably the most famous unknown unknown in recent history, but the financial world is full of them. The markets are always finding new ways to take investors by surprise, both on the downside and the upside.

As the 2008-2009 meltdown reminded us, financial risk is not limited to the stock market. In *The Black Swan*, Mr. Taleb laments the inadequacy of risk management in commercial banks and pokes fun of bankers, generally "dull" middle-aged men who are "clean-shaven and dress in possibly the most comforting and boring manner, in dark suits, white shirts, and red ties."

This conservatism, Taleb insists, is purely superficial:

> Similarly, think of a bank chairman whose institution makes steady profits over a long time, only to lose everything in a single reversal of fortune… There is no way to gauge the effectiveness of their lending activity by observing it over a day, a week, a month, or… even a century! In the summer of 1982, large American banks lost close to all their past earnings (cumulatively), about everything they had ever made in the history of American banking—everything. They had been lending to South and Central American countries that all defaulted at the same time— "an event of an exceptional nature." So it took just one summer to figure out that this was

a sucker's business and that all their earnings came from a very risky game. All the while the bankers led everyone, especially themselves, into believing they were "conservative."

Just as was the case with the record banking profits in the years leading up to the mortgage meltdown of 2008, the banking profits of the early 1980s "were simply cash borrowed from destiny with some random payback time."

Sadly, it is when we believe that we have been the most successful and that we are being the most conservative that we might in fact be taking the biggest risks!

## The Wild and Unexpected

The financial meltdown created quite a few "impossible" events. On Friday, October 24, 2008, the *Financial Times* reported that "swap spreads turned negative." It would be easy to dismiss this headline as just another bit of media noise except for one little technicality: **according to all of the rules of finance, it is a mathematical impossibility.** A negative swap spread means that the Treasury yield is higher than that of a swap of a similar maturity. As the "risk free" rate in virtually all financial models, the Treasury should always give the lowest taxable yield without exception. The pricing in the swaps market implies that the private issuers of swaps are somehow less risky than the U.S. government! Of course, this is absurd. All doubts about the fiscal responsibility of the government aside, no private company can ever be less risky than the U.S. government. With unlimited ability to tax and, if need be, print the needed money, a sovereign government by definition cannot default on debts denominated in its own currency.

Meanwhile, at the same time on the other side of the Atlantic, we found another absurd anomaly. **German automaker Volkswagen briefly became the most valuable company in the world!** A rush of panicked short covering caused the stock to *triple* in one day before finally easing to a lower, albeit still grossly overvalued, price. Short sellers of Volkswagen found themselves wiped out... in the middle of an economic contraction that has decimated the auto industry and eventually caused the bankruptcy of General Motors and Chrysler.

Does this sound like a rational or efficient market to you? Yeah, me neither. Yet all mainstream investment tools make the assumption that the markets are a model of rationality.

## The Nuts and Bolts of Modern Finance

Sometimes it can be useful to step back and ask an obvious question? Why exactly do we invest? The answer, of course, is to make money. When we invest, we expect to earn a return on our investment. If we put our money in the bank, we expect to earn interest, even if the rate is a little on the low side. We also know, with absolutely certainly, what our returns will be on our bank savings. The same is not true of stock market investments, of course. In the stock markets, you can experience a wide spectrum of returns, including some years with substantial losses—like 2008—or extraordinary gains—like 2009. Our reward for putting our capital at risk in the stock market—our "risk premium" in financial parlance—is the possibility of larger returns than would be earned on "risk free" alternatives, like Treasury bonds or a CD at the bank.

This is where it starts to get messy. How do you estimate what stock returns will be? Well, that's the problem. There is no reliable way to estimate future stock returns. So, standard industry practice is to simply take the average of past returns and use that as an estimate for the future. Professor Jeremy Siegel—whom I mentioned in previous chapters—calculated that over history stocks have returned 9%, before taking into account the effects of inflation. However, we also know that it is uncommon for the large-company stock index ever *actually* to earn 9% (only twice in the last 80 years has the S&P 500 index been within 1% of this number). Given that stocks rarely return their "expected" return, we instead estimate the likelihood that stock returns will fall within a certain range around our "expected" 9%. Mainstream investment analysis assumes that returns are distributed in what is called a **normal distribution**—or **bell curve. Figure 10.1** shows a normal distribution for annual stock market returns.

A normal distribution assumes that all of the data points are *independent* (like the idea that sequential rolls of dice are unrelated to each other) and that the observations are distributed *identically*. In other words, a bad year does not cause the next year to be good, and a good year does not cause the next year also to be good. Again, using the dice analogy, rolling snake eyes on your first roll does not make it any more likely that your next roll will be double sixes.

Of course, when it comes to investing, we know this is not true. Returns *are* dependent on prior returns, and anyone familiar with the markets knows that they can go through days, weeks, or even months of extreme turbulence—think 2008!—followed by long stretches of relative calm.

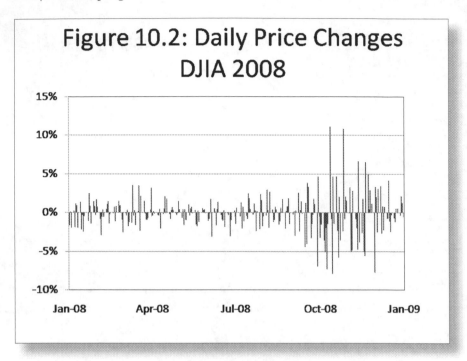

Figure 10.2: Daily Price Changes DJIA 2008

Figure 10.3: Daily Price Changes DJIA 1928-2010

**Figure 10.2** plots the daily returns of the Dow Jones Industrial Average in 2008. The chart should quickly dispel any belief that returns are independent or identically distributed. Taking a longer view, **Figure 10.3** plots daily returns from October 1928 to the present. For most of the history of the US stock market, daily volatility has been relatively small and uniform with only a few larger-the-usual moves, as a normal distribution would predict. However, the late 1920s and the 1930s tell a very different story. In those years, daily moves of more than 10% were pretty common. One data point truly stands out: ***October 19, 1987, the day the Dow fell 23%.***

If investment returns really do follow a normal distribution pattern, then the 1987 crash never should have happened—never, not once in a billion years. The problem is that the stock market is full of "once every billion years" days, even though we have only about 80 to 100 years' worth of reliable data. So, what does that actually mean? Suffice it to say that mainstream investment tools are flawed.

To illustrate how non-normal the stock market really is, I plotted the returns from Figure 10.3 on the normal distribution to see where they fall (**Figure 10.4**).

As you can see, Figure 10.4 is full of observations in the extreme ends of the bell curve. This type of chart is referred to as a normal distribution with **"fat tails,"** which means that extreme moves are far more common than the financial services industry assumes.

# Figure 10.4: Stock Returns
## Normal Distribution Assumed

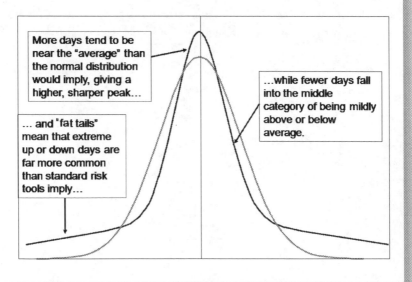

# Figure 10.5: Leptokurtosis vs. Normal

**Figure 10.5** illustrates the difference between a normal distribution and a fat-tailed distribution, more technically called "leptokurtic." Leptokurtic distributions can vary in terms of the fatness of the tails and the pointedness of the peak. The actual distribution of historical stock returns is a little less exaggerated than Figure 10.5 would suggest, but the point is to show you that there is a clear difference between the models and reality.

## Dealing with Risk and Return

No one complains about making too much money. While saving too much can impact your current standard of living, it is not what we would think of as a problem. The other end of the spectrum, saving too little, is all too common. When it comes to retirement, most of us are trying to figure out how to plan for the unknowable, which is how long we will live and how much it will cost. Once we have rough estimates of these two things, which is hard enough, then comes the second daunting task: determining how much to save. Simply put, the amount we need to save is based on how much we think we will need, how many years we can invest, and how much we think we will earn on our investment. It takes a lot of homework to make several of these estimates, but the last one, how much we will earn, is anybody's guess. Not only do extreme returns occur more frequently than we think, but they have long-lasting implications for our portfolio decisions. For this reason, income is a particularly valuable part of a portfolio. Income in the form of dividends and interest is real income, not ephemeral capital gains, hence the old market maxim "A bird in hand is worth two in the bush." Or as Tom Cruise and Cuba Gooding, Jr. screamed in *Jerry Maguire*, "Show me the *money*!"

## Lessons Not Learned During the Crisis

People underestimate the power of the market to induce amnesia in the masses. The worst financial meltdown in 100 years is a recent painful memory, yet investors are already back to business as usual. I have found that people's memory is about 18 months. 2008 was excruciatingly painful for everyone. However, I probably have a better memory of it because I was on the front lines and I can remember the actual mental and physical toll. Getting calls from clients for comfort, reporters for quotes and cable news outlets for analysis, sometimes as many as four a day. The pain is fresh. However, in general, it appears that we are hard wired to *not* learn our lessons. With that said, here is James Montier's Top Ten List of lessons not learned (all quotes are directly from Montier's white paper):[31]

## Lesson 1: Markets aren't efficient.

"As I have observed previously, the Efficient Market Hypothesis (EMH) is the financial equivalent of Monty Python's Dead Parrot. No matter how many times you point out that it is dead, believers insist it is just resting."

Montier is on to something here. While many in the profession have come to accept the obvious—that markets are neither efficient nor rational—the academic establishment has been reluctant to let it go. It's understandable; despite the theory's failings, there is more than 50 years of accumulated research, and a repudiation of the theory would mean that some of the leading academics spent their entire careers figuratively chasing their tails.

## Lesson 2: Relative performance is a dangerous game.

The key question in the investment management industry is not, "How much money did you make me?" or "How much money did you *save* me by being out of the market?" but rather "Did you beat the market?"

But does this kind of thinking really make sense? Does it make sense to benchmark every portfolio to the S&P 500 or a similar index? Doesn't this encourage the manager to take excessive risk and then blame "the market" if it doesn't pan out?

Relative performance creates perverse incentives for investment managers. As Montier writes, "Put in our terms, many (if not most) investment managers are more worried about career risk (losing your job) or business risk (losing funds under management) than they are about doing the right thing!"

Montier knows a little something about that. His firm, GMO, lost a good deal of its assets because Jeremy Grantham steadfastly refused to buy tech stocks during the dot com craze of the late 1990s. Grantham was ultimately proven right, and the investors that stuck with him avoided the bear market of 2000-2002 and made great money in years that followed. But in the interim, Grantham's firm suffered for doing the right thing.

## Lesson 3: The time is never different.

I dedicated an entire chapter to this concept, but frankly, Montier explains it better than I do:

> Contrary to the protestations of the likes of Greenspan, Bernanke, and Brown, bubbles can be diagnosed before they burst; they are *not* black swans. **The black swan defense is nothing more than an attempt to abdicate responsibility**. A good working knowledge of the history of bubbles can help preserve your capital. Ben Graham argued that an investor should "have an adequate idea of stock market history, in terms, particularly, of the major fluctuations. With this background he may be in a position to form some worthwhile judgment of the attractiveness or dangers... of the market." Nowhere is an appreciation of history more important than in the understanding of bubbles.

Well said, Mr. Montier.

## Lesson 4: Valuation matters.

Buy low and sell high. It sounds simple, doesn't it? Yet few seem to get this right. Instead, investors—both retail and professional—tend to chase growth and pay too much for it. Whether it's stocks, Miami condos, or gold, investors tend to pile in only *after* an asset has had a good run. Alas, humans are herd animals. Montier's comments here are quite insightful:

> At its simplest, value investing tells us to buy when assets are cheap and to avoid purchasing expensive assets. This simple statement seems so self-evident that it is hardly worth saying. Yet repeatedly I've come across investors willing to undergo mental contortions to avoid the valuation reality... Buying when markets are cheap generates significantly better returns

than buying when markets are expensive. Of course, the flip side is that one must be prepared to not be fully invested when the returns implied by equity pricing are exceptionally unattractive.

## Lesson 5: Wait for the fat pitch.

"Warren Buffett often speaks of the importance of waiting for the fat pitch—that perfect moment when patience is rewarded as the ball meets the sweet spot. However, most investors seem unable to wait, forcing themselves into action at every available opportunity, swinging at every pitch, as it were."

There is something about baseball that makes it uniquely suited for investment metaphors, and the idea of waiting for the fat pitch is certainly one of them. Warren Buffett made out like a bandit during the meltdown because he had cash at his disposal at a time when *everyone* wanted and needed cash. He made emergency loans to Goldman Sachs and General Electric at what amounted to pawn shop rates of interest because he waited for the fat pitch. The lesson here: don't waste your strikes swinging at subpar investments!

## Lesson 6: Sentiment matters.

"Investor returns are not only affected by valuation. Sentiment also plays a part. It is a cliché that markets are driven by fear and greed, but it is also disturbingly close to the truth. Sentiment swings like a pendulum, from irrational exuberance to the depths of despair."

Sometimes investing in the market can seem like carrying on a conversation with a crazy person. Benjamin Graham joked about this as far back as the 1930s, personifying the stock market as "Mr. Market," a wildly manic depressive gentleman who offers to sell his inventory at a bargain price one day and a ridiculously inflated price the next.

## Lesson 7: Leverage can't make a bad investment good, but it can make a good investment bad!

Never were truer words spoken. The real tragedy of the 2008 meltdown is that the basic business model—pooling and securitizing mortgage loans—is actually quite good. But when you added in irresponsible lending practices and then turbocharged the entire thing with insane amounts of leverage… well, it became a ticking time bomb. This is what blew up Long-Term Capital Management a decade before. Had the professors not been leveraged 40-to-1, they could have waited out the period of volatility. They'd probably still be in business. Unfortunately, debt is like crack cocaine for the investment industry, and it's an almost impossible addiction to break. As Montier writes,

> Leverage is a dangerous beast. It can't ever turn a bad investment good, but it can turn a good investment bad. Simply piling leverage onto an investment with a small return doesn't transform it into a good idea. Leverage has a darker side from a value perspective as well: it has the potential to turn a good investment into a bad one! Leverage can limit your staying power, and transform a temporary impairment (i.e., price volatility) into a permanent impairment of capital.

## Lesson 8: Over-quantification hides real risk.

This is something I discussed earlier in this chapter. At its root, investing is not complicated. Warren Buffett—the best in the business—went years without having even a single computer in his office. This is not to say it's *easy*. If it were, we would all be Warren Buffett!

The current obsession with quantifying everything does make the business unnecessarily complicated, however, and it distorts the idea of what risk really is—a concept, not a precise number. Montier does a good job of explaining this:

> Finance has turned the art of transforming the simple into the perplexing into an industry. Nowhere (at least outside of academia) is overly complex structure and elegant (but not robust) mathematics so beloved. The reason for this obsession with needless complexity is clear: it is far easier to charge higher fees for things that sound complex.
>
> Two of my investing heroes were cognizant of the dangers posed by elegant mathematics. Ben Graham wrote: "Mathematics is ordinarily considered as producing precise and dependable results; but in the stock market the more elaborate and abstruse

the mathematics the more uncertain and speculative are the conclusions we draw there from... Whenever calculus is brought in, or higher algebra, you could take it as a warning that the operator was trying to substitute theory for experience, and usually also to give to speculation the deceptive guise of investment."

The key insight here is the substituting of theory for experience. Theory is important, of course. It's what helps us understand what is happening in the markets. But you have to keep a sense of perspective, and it's pretty obvious that this was lost in the run-up to the 2008 meltdown.

## Lesson 9: Macro matters.

Some readers might remember the old Miller Lite commercials in which the world was divided in two camps—those that believed the beer tasted great and those that believed it was less filling. The closest thing in the world of investments to this kind of thinking would be the debate over which investment approach is better: top-down, or bottom-up.

In a nutshell, the "top-down" approach resembles a funnel. This is the approach I generally take in my practice. I look at the overall economy and market conditions and make a judgment first on the market as a whole. I ask myself, "Do I even want to be in stocks based on economic conditions?" From there I will identify what areas or sectors will benefit in the current environment. On down the line, I focus on how much goes towards growth and how much towards value and so on until I find the best individual investments. This is the basis for my Top-Down Tactical™ investment strategy, which is the foundation of my firm's success.

In contrast, a "bottom-up" investor ignores the "noise" of current economic conditions and instead looks for investments that are attractively priced. This is how most forms of traditional value investing work, and under some market conditions it is safe to ignore the macro. But this would have been a disaster in the recent crisis. As Montier explains,

Ignoring the top-down can be extraordinarily expensive. The credit bust has been a perfect example of why understanding the top-down can benefit and inform the bottom-up. The last 12 months have been unusual for value investors as two clear camps emerged from their normally more homogenous whole. A schism over financials has split value investors into two diametrically opposed groups...

Essentially, the difference between these two camps comes down to an appreciation of the importance of the bursting of the credit bubble. Those who understood the impact of the bursting of such a bubble didn't go near financials. Those who focused more (and in some cases exclusively) on the bottom-up just saw cheapness, but missed the value trap arising from a bursting credit bubble. It often pays to remember the wise words of Jean-Marie Eveillard.

"Sometimes, what matters is not so much how low the odds are that circumstances would turn quite negative, what matters more is what the consequences would be if that happens." In terms of finance jargon, expected payoff has two components: expected return and probability. While the probability may be small, a truly appalling expected return can still result in a negative payoff.

Neither top-down nor bottom-up has a monopoly on insight. We should learn to integrate their dual perspectives.

Well said. In this business, one approach does not work best at all times. Focusing just on one school of thought is mental laziness, and we are not likely to be successful as investors when we go down that road.

## Lesson 10: Look for sources of cheap insurance.

"The final lesson that we should take from the 2008-09 experience is that insurance is often a neglected asset when it comes to investing. The cash flows associated with insurance often seem unappealing in a world when many seem to prefer 'blow up' (small gain, small gain... big loss) to 'bleed out' (small loss, small loss... big gain)."

It was this line of thinking that prompted me to create our TDT™ Protected Dividend Strategy. It combines our Top Down Tactical TDT™ with a protected dividend approach that captures the dividends and income of high yielding stocks, bonds and preferred stocks, while hedging the principle against a market decline—what I like to call, "Grabbing nickels and dimes in front of the steamroller."

Insurance today is quite expensive in some areas. One popular—though somewhat controversial—form of insurance is gold. Gold is generally a poor investment; it pays no dividends or interest and has no earnings. It's really nothing more than a shiny metal used to make trinkets. Yet at the right price, it can make sense to have a little gold in your portfolio as a hedge against currency and financial instability.

Buying gold today at its currently inflated prices ($1,400 at time of writing) would seem like a great example of closing the barn door after the horse has already bolted. Treasury securities would also appear to be a bit on the expensive side, though given the nonexistent level of inflation they might stay this way for a while.

I'm not quite as harsh on the investment management business as James Montier. The optimist in me believes that some of these lessons have indeed been learned, at least by the current generation of financiers. We'll have other bubbles and meltdowns, of course. Eventually, another one is bound to happen, and when they do we emerge a little older and a little wiser. The key for us as investors is to understand risk and to use that understanding to avoid these pitfalls as they come up. No investor misses every bear market or crash, but if you are able to miss even one or two big ones over the course of your investing career, it can make a major difference in your net worth.

# Chapter 11:

## Terror, War and Pregnancy

I want to take a little time here to discuss geopolitical risks because this is a topic that is misunderstood by many investors. We tend to fixate on the wrong things. Geopolitics *do* matter. But I've been in this business long enough to know that the things most people worry about—such as terrorism and small-scale conventional war—tend to have a surprisingly small effect on stock returns over time. A bigger issue is the longer-term reshaping of the world economy, as up-and-coming countries such as China and India gain ground at the expense of established powers like the United States and Europe. Demographics play a big part in these transformations, though the media tends to ignore this because it's too slow-moving to capture their attention.

Terror attacks can have a *big* effect on the market when they strike. Just think back to September 11, 2001. The New York Stock Exchange remained closed for almost a week, and when it finally reopened, all hell broke loose. The week that followed was one of the worst in the history of the U.S. stock market. But then, a funny thing happened. After finding a bottom in late September, the market turned around and proceeded to rise by almost 30% over the five months that followed.

Similarly, history buffs recall the Wall Street terror attack of 1920 in which an Italian anarchist bombed JP Morgan's headquarters, which sits directly across from the New York Stock Exchange. If you happen to be in New York, walk down Wall Street and take a look. You can still see the pock marks in the side of the building. Needless to say, the attack—which killed 38 and seriously injured another 143—did little to stop the Roaring Twenties and the stock market bubble that characterized that decade. Whether the anarchists liked it or not, the 1920s were one of the best decades in U.S. stock market history. It was the wild excesses of the investors themselves—and *not* any act of terror or war—that ultimately killed the market in the 1929 Crash.

Israel has spent most of its 60 years of statehood facing legitimate threats to its survival. By the early 1980s, Israel had made at least a fragile truce with its neighboring states, but this period marked the rise of Palestinian terrorism, which has continued off and on until the present. Despite this, Israel has developed a cutting-edge tech sector and a bustling stock market. Similarly, both Spain and the United Kingdom have had multiple decades of struggle with home-grown terror organizations in the Basque ETA and the Northern Irish IRA, yet their economies have grown and prospered, the sovereign debt crisis notwithstanding. The United States too had its homegrown terrorists in the form of Ku Klux Clan in the South and the various leftist terror groups of the 1960s and early 1970s like the Symbionese Liberation Army of Patty Hearst fame, yet this period saw an enormous boom in the stock market. And of course, no listing of American terrorism would be complete without mentioning the Timothy McVeigh attack in 1995—which, as terrifying as it was, did virtually nothing to slow down the economic boom that the country was enjoying at the time.

Though it is horrifying to see the aftermath of an attack, investors tend to have short memories, and the economy and financial markets have a way of recovering. Life does go on. Terrorism—abhorrent though it is—just doesn't matter that much past the short term.

But what about war? War is a little more complicated, of course. Its effects on the stock and bond markets depend on the country's chances of winning. The United States enjoyed a massive bull market throughout World War II and the years that followed. But Japan? Well, not so much.

A prolonged and exceptionally expensive war can sap investor enthusiasm. But again, not always. American stocks did not fare particularly well during the Vietnam War era, but this was due more to the rampant inflation and other economic dislocations of the era, not the *war*, per se. Returning to the 1990s again, former President Bill Clinton had a very militarily-active presidency, though none of his campaigns had much of an effect on the stock market.

In none of the examples mentioned above was the freedom or security of the United States at significant risk. None of these were wars for survival, not even World War II. The United States could afford to have a war or two go the wrong way because, for the most part, the wars were taking place far from our shores. Of course, if a war or disruptive attack were severe enough, your stock portfolio would be the last thing on your mind.

The Rise of China: What Does it Mean?

According to Steven Rosefielde and D. Quinn Mills, authors of *Masters of Illusion: American Leadership in the Media Age*:

> Woodrow Wilson made a basic mistake at the end of World War I and thereby contributed to the making of World War II. He believed that the dissatisfaction of minorities within polygot empires was the basic cause of the war (after all, didn't a Serbian nationalist assassinate the heir to the throne of the Austrian Empire and thereby occasion the war?) So he worked for the dissolution of the Austrian and European parts of the Russian empire, but left the German empire (made up of a single nationality) intact. Thus, he surrounded Germany with weak states, providing the temptation and opportunity for Hitler. We are in danger of doing the same now. We are taking our eyes off the great powers, and looking instead at issues like terrorism.

The greatest power in question is, of course, China. With the fall of the Berlin War and the discrediting of communist ideology, there was a popular belief that we had reached "The End of History," in Francis Fukuyama's words. With no more ideological divisions, capitalist liberal democracy would be the ruling order of the day. There would be rogue states, of course. But the days of great power rivalry were over. After all, the world's economies are intertwined. Coca-Cola is sold throughout the world, McDonald's is in 119 countries across six continents and we buy more foreign-made cars than our own. We're basically all on the same team now; why would we need to fight?

Long before the "isms" of the 19th and 20th centuries (communism, fascism, Nazism, etc.) there were rivalries between the monarchies and republican movements in Europe. Before that, there were wars of religion between Protestants and Catholics and between Christians and

Muslims. But before any of this, there were simple conflicts between states, kings, warlords or even between tribes for money, power and influence. This is the oldest form of great power rivalry, and it has always been a contributing factor to the ideological ones.

The problem with the Fukuyama argument is that pre-World War I Europe largely enjoyed similar conditions. The Continent was at peace and had largely been so since the close of the Napoleonic Wars in 1815. The royal families of Europe knew each other and most were related to one another ("inbred" might be a more accurate description, truth be told). Republican France had no axe to grind with its monarchical neighbors. This was the first golden age of globalization and free trade, and Europe was becoming wealthy—and it ended in an orgy of bloodshed in the worst war the world had ever seen.

So, is war with China inevitable? Absolutely not. But tensions are rising. With the United States distracted in the Middle East and with its domestic economic problems, China has become more assertive in other parts of the world. China is also quickly expanding its army and is building a blue-water navy. China's economy has also recently surpassed Japan's to become the second largest in the world. Whether or not we have war, we certainly have to deal with a more powerful and more assertive China.

## Are America's Days of Global Dominance Numbered?

It has become popular to speak of the decline of the West and of the United States in particular. Titles like Fareed Zakaria's *The Post-American World* have become commonplace. (While Zakaria's book was less about America's decline and more about "the rise of the rest," its gloomy title certainly fits the growing consensus.) Regardless of whether America is waxing or waning, we will undoubtedly have to make room at the table for some new, emerging powers.

The two most commonly cited "emerging powers," China and India, have populations that are both massive and rapidly expanding. Does this make them a shoe-in at the top of the heap? Though their size may be advantageous—demographics will be important to these coming shifts—innovation and technology will be the driving forces. After all, some of the greatest world powers in history were small, technologically-savvy nations or even small city-states. Looking back, it may be hard to believe that the British Empire, which straddled the globe, was administered by a small, rainy island in the North Atlantic.

Rome, the greatest empire of classical times, started out as an ambitious city. And well into the late Middle Ages, tiny Venice was the most powerful maritime country in Europe—and was the primary power holding the mighty Turkish Ottoman Empire at bay.

Neil Howe, who previously co-wrote several groundbreaking books on demographic trends with William Strauss (*Generations, The Fourth Turning, Millennials Rising*), published a new book in 2008 with Richard Jackson: *The Graying of the Great Powers: Demography and Geopolitics in the 21st Century*. What do Jackson and Howe have to say on the matter?

> The population and GDP of the United States, due to its relatively high fertility and immigration rates, will expand steadily as a share of the developed-world totals. In tandem, the influence of the United States within the developed world will likely rise. Many of today's multilateral theorists look forward to a global order in which the U.S. influence diminishes. In fact, any reasonable demographic projection points to a *growing* U.S. dominance among the developed nations that preside over this global order.

I would agree with Zakaria to an extent that the U.S. will need to find room at the table for up-and-comers like China, India and Brazil. But as Zakaria, Jackson, and Howe would all seem to agree, the United States will remain the preeminent economic, diplomatic and military force in the world for the foreseeable future.

Are Europe's Demographic Trends Reversible?

All demographers would agree that the West's and particularly Europe's low birthrates point to serious economic difficulties in the future. The question then becomes, are these demographic trends reversible? Or is Europe truly entering a demographic death spiral from which it will never recover? Some European countries have witnessed modest increases in their birthrates in recent years, even if the overall rate remains dangerously low. Jackson and Howe explain, "Notwithstanding the higher fertility rate of immigrants, most demographers do not believe that the recent uptick in fertility heralds a major turnaround in the long-term trend. In most countries, it appears to be the result of a temporary 'timing shift' that will soon run its course."

So as countries go through a period of modernization, the birth rate gets temporarily depressed due to women extending their educations and careers and postponing motherhood. A given woman may indeed still have the "normal" 2-3 kids over her lifetime; it's just that she gets started at 30 instead of 22.

Once this timing shift is complete, the fertility rate will recover to some extent. This is precisely what happened in the United States. Using Jackson and Howe's statistics, "after plunging from 3.7 in the mid-1950s to 1.7 in the mid 1970s, the U.S. fertility rate rose to 2.0 by the early 1990s under the impact of late-birthing baby boomers, where it has remained ever since."

In some of the European countries with the lowest fertility rates, such as Spain, Italy and Greece, it is likely that the timing shift is not yet complete. These traditionally "macho" countries started the process much later. So, each of these countries may enjoy a mini baby boom as this first generation of post-traditional women finally have children. But, as Jackson and Howe continue, "the potential to raise fertility is limited. In the United States, baby boomers only recuperated a fraction of the births in their 30s and 40s that they did not have in their 20s— and European women are unlikely to fare much better."

Spain, Italy and Greece may return to something close to the replacement rate of 2.1 children per woman from their current apocalyptically low rates of around 1.3. But the days of the large Mediterranean family are most likely over.

Can Pro-Natal Policies — Such as Child Tax
Credits — Make a Difference?

The evidence is pretty convincing that pro-natal policies are largely ineffective in the modern, consumer-oriented economy. When the cultural and economic climate changes from one that favors a large family to one that favors a small family, there is not much the government can do about it. Will a child tax credit of a couple thousand dollars compensate a parent for the tens or hundreds of thousands of dollars in direct expenses? What about the untold thousands of dollars in lost wages and career opportunities (particularly for women who get "mommy tracked")? And what about lifestyle issues, such as the ability to take an unplanned trip to the Caribbean? The obvious answer is no; people who decide to have children believe that doing so has nonmonetary benefits, and government incentives are not a major factor in their decision. This is what Jackson and Howe have to say on the matter:

> Until recently, ideal fertility—that is the number of children that women say is optimal—remained at or above replacement in every developed country, even as actual fertility rates fell far beneath it. This suggested that there might be room for a substantial rebound if more supportive policies simply allowed women to actualize their ideal. But in a growing number of countries, including Austria, Italy, and Germany, ideal fertility has now dropped well beneath replacement. What has happened, according to some demographers, is that young adults in today's lowest-fertility countries, having spent their entire lives in societies where children are rare, have acquired a "culture of low fertility."

Despite this, Jackson and Howe strongly recommend aggressive pro-natal policies such as those used in France and the Scandinavian countries. It is fair to ask: given the seriousness of the problem, doesn't it make sense to give it a try?

## What Effects Will Aging Demographics Have on the Culture and Economy?

As you might expect, younger societies are full of dynamism, which is manifested by risk taking and an optimistic outlook. An older society, in contrast, becomes more conservative and risk averse. Productivity, progress and mobility slow. This has been Japan's experience and it fits neatly into Jackson and Howe's theory. They continue:

> When economists and historians try to describe the special economic vitality that often characterizes eras of high versus low population growth—the nineteenth century versus the fifteenth century in Europe, for example, for example, or 1960s versus the 1930s—they often allude to a contrast in a mood that cannot be reduced to a strictly classical analysis of the production function. The classical analysis, indeed, usually argues that a stationary or declining population should

translate into economic performance (by lifting the ration of labor to land and to other fixed natural resources). Yet eras of high population growth have their own special attributes that are harder to define within standard theory—a restlessness mobility, urgency and optimism.

Note: I argued against this classical view earlier in this book in my discussion of Gregory Clark's *A Farewell to Alms* and David Hackett Fischer's *The Great Wave*. Continuing with Jackson and Howe,

> John Maynard Keynes and his U.S. counterpart Alvin H. Hansen always emphasized the role of population growth in triggering what Keynes called the "animal spirits" of investors. John Hicks, in his famous review of Keynes' General Theory, remarked: "Expectation of a continually expanding market, made possible by increasing population, is a fine thing for keeping up the spirits of entrepreneurs. With increasing population investment can go roaring ahead, even if invention is rather stupid; increasing population is therefore actually favorable to employment... *Perhaps the whole Industrial Revolution of the last two hundred years has been nothing else but a vast secular boom, largely induced by the unparalleled rise in population.*"

The modern economy depends on population growth. For an economy to grow, it needs more spenders. That's what we had in the 1980s and 1990s with the baby boomers. However, when a nation transforms from net spender to net saver, as the U.S. has been doing since the early 2000s, its economy contracts. To give a simplistic example, how can Ford sell more cars when there are fewer people of driving age to sell to? The only modern economy that has ever dealt with an aging and shrinking population is, of course, Japan. And as Japan's recent experience has shown, there is no real solution to this problem. There is no substitute for people.

Parting Thoughts

Richard Jackson and Neil Howe are not revolutionary in their writing of *The Graying of the Great Powers;* they are certainly not reinventing the wheel of demographic analysis. That said, *Graying* is an excellent collection of statistics and solid analysis of the major demographic issues that will shape the decades to come. For readers looking for a "big picture" book that will help them in their understanding of the world—and possibly their investments as well—Jackson and Howe's latest deserves a place on the bookshelf.

As investors, it is good to understand geopolitical trends, of course. Even though demographics tend to be more important from a macro perspective, whoever comes up with the next great technological innovation or has the most innovators will lead the world in the future. That is precisely why you see a big push for "green" industries and clean technology. That's one of the possible industries that will employ millions of people, thus providing an economic boom for their country. In the short term however, it ultimately all comes down to the price you pay: at a given price, are you being properly compensated for the risk you are taking? In the next chapter, I'll go into some of the details of my wealth management practice. At the risk of giving away some of my trade secrets, I'll explain my processes and offer insight on how to best approach your own investments.

# Chapter 12:

# How to Make Money in this Market

There is little doubt that we are in an economic pickle for the next several years, which will foster an extended period of low inflation and possibly outright deflation. In fact, without the magnitude of government intervention through economic stimulus, deflation would already be prevalent. This is very much contrary to the pervading view these days, but the research speaks for itself.

Even today, Ben Bernanke and his financial puppeteers (the guys who are printing the money) are telling us to take our money out of savings and invest it, or be guaranteed a loss (after inflation and taxes). They are keeping rates low to force you to invest your money.

Only a flexible, active allocation has been demonstrated to add true value over market cycles. A static allocation or a "buy-and-hold" approach simply rides higher on the incoming tide and falls along with the outgoing tide. You are effectively trusting your financial future to the whims of an uncertain market. It's a lot like playing a game of craps. Your fortune will go up and it will go down, and the timing on when you need to walk away from the table will decide how much money you have left. The proof is in the pudding, as this approach got crushed during the recent crisis and has little to show for the past 10-12 years, now called the "lost decade."

In sharp contrast, a "hands-on tactical" or active allocation approach, much like our Top-Down Tactical TDT™ strategy, seeks to outperform during rising markets by being invested in the leading asset classes and avoiding the laggards that drain performance, and then preserve those gains during the inevitable market declines by having a defensive risk management and exit strategy.

In this kind of economic environment, investors must employ an active tactical approach to investing. Old fashioned buy-and-hold, which I like to call *buy-and-hope*, is dead. Only during prolonged periods of bull markets can this approach work and that is clearly not our environment today or any time soon. That strategy really is your grandfather's Oldsmobile.

In a tactical approach, you may have a baseline portfolio allocation, but you're certainly not married to it. Instead, you have the ability to shift your money between asset classes or out of the markets altogether as conditions warrant. Going to cash can save you a lot of headaches *and* heart attacks. Even in the worst of long-term bear markets, there are stretches where certain sectors or the market as a whole do quite well. Using a tactical approach, you can participate in market rallies while sitting out some of the bear market corrections.

Let me give you a practical example. During the most intense moments of the recent crisis, I spent day and night (I couldn't sleep anyway) focusing on how to take advantage of the situation. What transpired was perhaps the greatest set of trades I have made in my career. I began buying the bonds and preferred stocks of companies the day it was announced that they were recipients of TARP funds.

I knew there were risks involved in the trade, but the risks were calculated. After all, risk must be managed properly, not avoided, otherwise you will not only always guarantee yourself a loss to purchasing power, but you will never get to take advantage of good opportunities as they come along. My thought was that once the government became a company's partner, so to speak, they would not be allowed to fail. Sure, the stockholders may languish, but that was not my concern. I owned the *bonds and preferred stock*, not the regular common stock, and as long as the company simply survived, my clients would collect their interest payments and get their principal return.

So, with the help my gifted bond trader Mike, I embarked on buying these TARP recipient company bonds and preferreds for clients. I took large positions in Goldman Sachs, American Express, HSBC, Bank of America and GMAC. I didn't have to buy securities with long maturities—usually just 2-4 years—and I was locking in yields of 15—

20%. With the preferreds I received the same yield as well as a big kicker as the prices of these doubled or tripled. Wow, what a coup. I still get goose bumps today when I think about it.

Although situations like these are few and far between, it's important to keep a sharp eye out for these types of opportunities, or work with someone who does and knows what to look for. In this current environment, you do *not* want investments that depend solely on rising prices. This includes most "growth stocks" as well as real estate and commodities.

As for what *does* work in a period of extremely low inflation or deflation, I have a one-word answer: **income.** After all, if you are not collecting some form of income from your investments, you are at the whim of the market. When prices are stagnant or falling, the income received from a stable investment like bonds, dividend-paying stocks, MLPs, REITs or annuities become all the more attractive. Pay yourself first.

The process that I go through when building an individual financial plan is very structured and disciplined. I take a holistic approach to wealth management for each individual client, never taking a one-size-fits-all or swing-for-the-fences approach. Wealth management is a comprehensive life plan, incorporating all the phases of your life and your family's life, whether you intend to spend every last nickel, give what's left to the kids or donate it to charity. My goal here is to build a financial plan that takes the very least amount of risk possible to reach its goals.

Step One: Determine the Required Rate of Return

As Yogi Berra once quipped, "If you don't know where you are going, you will wind up somewhere else." If you don't know what rate of return you are targeting, how will you know if your portfolio is appropriate and if your overall strategy is working? Frequently investors incorrectly compare their success to an index like the Dow Jones Industrial Average or the S&P 500. Most people do not want or need all the risk that the stock market possesses, nor should they take it. Often times investors simply need to keep pace with purchasing power (inflation and taxes), yet they subject themselves to sleepless nights and broken dreams by taking on more risk than they think they need. Determining your *required* rate of return is the most crucial step.

In order to reach this number, we work backward starting with your end goal in mind. We know how much money you have today; that part is easy. After putting a pencil to it, we calculate how much you need to have at crucial points in your life. After figuring the number of years you have to reach that point, the rate of return you need to meet your needs becomes an easy "plug-in" number.

As you get closer to retirement, downside protection with an exit strategy becomes critical. It becomes effectively impossible to make the money back if you lose it to a major bear market, a correction or a supposedly rare black swan event. Invest for need, not for greed.

## Step Two: Determine the Risk Tolerance

After determining your required rate of return, the focus turns to the subject of risk. Specifically, how much risk we must assume in order to reach our required return. The answer is simply to take the very least amount of risk necessary to achieve your objectives. Period. Greed always takes over when we think about how much we "could" make if everything went perfectly. It's often not until the market crashes do we realize that we are taking too much risk.

## Step Three: Determine the Broad Allocation

The goal of allocation optimization is to find the portfolio which offers the highest expected return for a given amount of risk or the least amount of risk for a given level of return. I spent my early years with brokerage firms that heavily influenced and kept strict control over what we invested in and taught us to invest in stocks, bonds and cash— and to stay invested. That was it! There wasn't much discussion about alternative investments. I also recall that an aggressive portfolio had something like 85% in stocks and a moderate to aggressive portfolio had 70% in stocks. There was no personal attention whatsoever. In fact, you see many people today get swayed by these so called "personal portfolio management" programs which are nothing more than glorified mutual funds. In a true customized investment plan, your portfolio must be tailor-made for your personal situation with regards to everything from risk to taxes, and each holding must be just right for you individually.

Of course, no one really complains when their portfolio makes too much money. But if you were holding that much in stocks when the recent bear came knocking, your portfolio got mauled. Moreover, if you lost 50% in a year, you would need to earn 100% just to break even. Therefore, in my view, managing the downside risk is the single most important thing I can do for my client's portfolio. *Any plan must have a personal exit strategy.* Unfortunately many investors learned this the hard way in the recent crisis.

Therefore, in portfolio construction, I search for assets with a good risk/return relationship and a low correlation to each other, as well as assets with a low correlation to the broader stock market. My ultimate goal is to find the combination of assets that protects well on the downside and lets the upside take care of itself.

Keep in mind, if you have sufficient assets to build your own fund, you should do so. For many investors, and certainly for wealthy investors, you should avoid owning traditional mutual funds, except for special situations such as for specific short-term sector allocations. Mutual funds have tremendous disadvantages. They are illiquid because they are only priced once a day. There are "gotcha" phantom taxes on gains, an added layer of fees and no personal management to represent your financial interests.

In short, I build my client's own personal no-load fund. There are no fees in or out, no commissions on stock or bond transactions, and if we use a mutual fund there are never any loads. If the fund has a load, the load is waived. This puts me on the same team as my client.

Step Four: Select the Subcategories

After we determine the broad allocation, we must choose the subcategories. Most of us are taught early to diversify over a number of categories. What I've learned is that simple diversification alone does not necessarily protect in a major panic like 2008. You have to stay nimble and tactical, and part of that is choosing the right mix of subcategories.

- **Stocks.** I favor different categories or sectors depending on economic and market conditions. Once it's decided as to how much will be allocated to stocks, the next allocation is made towards how much goes into each sector: large, mid, small cap, value, growth or blend. I often use ETFs as they provide the ability to select a specific sector and sub-sector that do not correlate with the other sectors. Too often people believe they are diversified just by owning a lot of stocks or mutual funds only to find out that they correlate too much or the funds all own the same underlying stocks. Your investments must adapt to changing market conditions. I also will get out of *all* stocks and into cash during dangerous periods.

- **Bonds.** For bonds, I invest in the best after-tax returns with the shortest maturities available. My goal here is to achieve a positive return with the bonds no matter how interest rates are trending. Currently I'm getting close to double digit yields in short term bonds with maturities of just five years, so why take the risk that comes with longer-dated bonds?

- **Alternative Investments.** Although real estate in the form of real estate investments trusts (REITs) could easily be included in the stock category, I use it here. Others include managed futures, Master Limited Partnerships with dividends that are 85% tax-free, currency ETFs, options (especially covered calls), commodity funds and ETFs, and long-short or market neutral funds. I am seeking assets that are not highly correlated with the broader stock market.

Step Six: Select the Specific Holdings

In selecting the specific holdings, I have many tools at my disposal that are not available to individuals or are cost prohibitive for many of them, such as: the institutional version of Morningstar Office; Lowry's Independent Research, which has been around since 1938 and provides the best technical analysis I know of; Bloomberg; Allocation Master; Zacks and JPMorgan research to name just a few. My 25+ years in the business allows me to find things that others can't. The specifics will depend directly on the current economic and market environment, and my outlook for the short, intermediate and long term.

Step Seven: Implement the Portfolio

Tactical asset allocation is hands-on portfolio management that over-weights and under-weights different market allocations based on market conditions, as well as utilizing cash during dangerous times. A buy-and-hold asset allocation style dictates buying many investment categories and holding them regardless of market conditions. I think that's ludicrous. Our trademarked **Top-Down Tactical (TDT™) investment management strategy** is built for today's economic environment.

Step Eight: Monitor the Portfolio

When monitoring the portfolio I constantly examine the broad allocation as well as the underlying holdings. Although I conduct comprehensive client reviews quarterly, I am constantly monitoring each account. The bottom line to me is the advisor's version of the Hippocratic Oath, "Provide safety, security and peace of mind."

The Joy of Dividends

Dividends are essential for every serious investor. Speculators don't need them, gamblers wouldn't touch them, but genuine long-term investors can't live without them. Dividends have accounted for almost 50% of the S&P 500's returns since 1925 and over 100% for the last decade.

Though the focus of this section is stock dividends, the analysis is applicable for all income-oriented investments, be they common stocks, preferred stocks, REITs, bonds or just about any investment that enhances its return by distributing capital back to its investors. These investments do well when the market does well, but more importantly they outperform when the stock market is either flat or down, providing steady income and downside protection. Capital gains can be ephemeral; income is *real*.

Investors who ignore dividends are essentially gambling. As I previously mentioned, building a portfolio of investments that does not provide any income is not too different from playing craps. You will go up, you will go down, and the timing of when you walk away from the table (i.e., needing the money to retire) will decide how much money you have. Pity the poor retirees of the last decade, because if they needed their money to live on over the last 10–12 years, it is likely that their retirement dreams—along with their portfolios—have vanished.

Preferred stock is an asset class many investors do not understand. Preferred stock may be a great investment option for income, but the word "stock" in the name is often misleading. Although these "stocks" can trade on the major stock exchanges, they are really fixed-income investments that have more in common with bonds or CDs than with common stocks. The dividend payments for preferred stocks are set when the shares are issued and generally do not vary. Most of them become callable five years after they are issued. This means that if interest rates fall, a company can take back the shares and pay you the price at which they were issued.

Many analysts agree that one of the positives of preferreds has been their relatively stable share price, although they do fluctuate. That stability comes from knowing the level of future dividends, as long as the companies continue to meet all of their debt obligations. With common stock, by contrast, companies can cut dividends during lean times without any warning. Generally, preferreds are susceptible to the same risk factors as bonds, like inflation and rising interest rates. For the most part, if a company misses earnings estimates, that might affect the common stock, but not the preferreds. However, if a company is at legitimate risk of financial distress or bankruptcy, even preferred dividends can be cut. This happened to several companies in 2008, and investors who believed their investments were conservative got a rude awakening.

For the individual investor, preferreds are generally easier to own than individual bonds. Preferreds can be bought and sold on the major exchanges through virtually any broker, rather than in the bond market, which is less liquid and transparent. And shares are usually priced at $25 each when they are issued, versus the $1,000 price for most new corporate bonds.

For tax purposes, there are two flavors of preferred stocks. Many preferreds have dividends that are eligible for the qualified dividend tax rate—15 percent for most investors—because the dividends are paid with after-tax dollars, while others pay dividends that are taxed at an investor's federal income tax rate. The companies write off these payments, so from the perspective of the IRS, they are more like the interest that is paid to corporate bondholders.

Sometimes preferreds do not pay qualified dividends but yield a bit more than those that do, so these may be better to hold in tax-advantaged accounts like IRAs. However, if the dividend is high enough even after you pay the taxes, as is often the case, a non-retirement account is just fine. After all, it's not what you make but what you keep that counts. If you are buying an individual security, the prospectus will say whether it pays qualified dividends.

Preferred stocks can be a great addition to your portfolio, whether you are looking to get a higher yield than CDs or money markets, or to provide stability to your portfolio in a volatile market.

A Man from a Different Time

James Montier of GMO has done excellent work on common stock dividends. I recommend you browse his recent white paper "A Man from a Different Time," available for free on the GMO website (www. gmo.com). In this section, I am going to share with you some of the insights from that paper.

In doing an exhaustive study of stock returns going back to 1871, Montier reached several conclusions. Some are obvious, but others will likely come as a surprise to you. In a given year, nearly 80% of the real total return is generated by changes in stock valuation, with the remainder coming from the dividend yield and the growth rate of dividends (see Figure 12.1). This makes sense, of course. Stock prices regularly have intra-year swings of 30% or more. As your time horizon expands, however, fundamentals like dividends become far more important. Montier found that at even a short five-year time horizon, it is dividend yield and dividend growth that account for almost 80% of the return, with changes in valuation accounting for barely 20%.

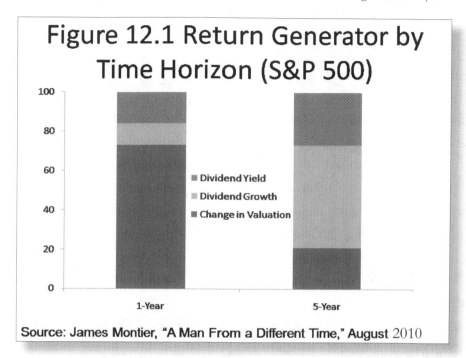

Figure 12.1 Return Generator by Time Horizon (S&P 500)

Source: James Montier, "A Man From a Different Time," August 2010

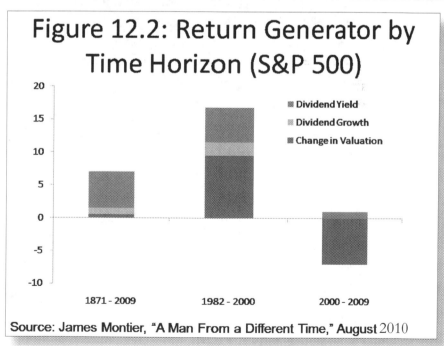

Figure 12.2: Return Generator by Time Horizon (S&P 500)

Source: James Montier, "A Man From a Different Time," August 2010

Over longer periods, **dividends account for a full 90% of real total returns** (see the first bar on Figure 12.2). Interestingly, something changed during the 1982–2000 period. During this "cult of equity" period in which the Baby Boomers accumulated their investment nest eggs, dividends were deemphasized in favor of share buybacks, acquisitions or the accumulation of cash on corporate balance sheets. Capital gains became the primary driver of investor returns, which made sense for tax reasons but which also led to the rise of a gambling mentality that has since wreaked havoc on the market.

Of course, for everything there is a season. Dividends were the *only* source of return during the 2000–2009 period. Stock price returns were *negative* for the period.

What are we to take away from all of this? Though tax policy will have an effect on returns going forward, dividends should be a major focus of your investment strategy whether you are a young investor just beginning to accumulate assets or an experienced investor in or nearing retirement. That is simply where the sweet spot is in the current market, providing the best returns with the least risk possible.

If you don't need the income now for current needs, reinvest your dividends to accelerate the compounding process. By doing this, you raise the odds that you can generate respectable returns even in a bear market. Dividend reinvestment is a form of dollar-cost averaging, and corrections and bear markets actually work to your advantage over time. If the value of your shares suffers a short-term setback, your dividend payments allow you to buy more shares at a cheaper price.

As always, use common sense. Investors who chased high dividends in the form of banks, finance companies and business development companies saw much of their investment wiped out in 2008. Never buy a stock simply because the dividend yield is high, but always consider the dividend as a major source of long-term returns.

If It's Good Enough for Chairman Bernanke...

Though Chairman Bernanke has become a controversial figure in the wake of the bank bailouts of 2008 and 2009, most of us would be curious to know what the most powerful man in the financial world had in his personal investment portfolio.

Before he became Fed Chairman, Ben Bernanke had to disclose his financial holdings. As you might expect, most of his liquid wealth was in fairly generic stock and bond mutual funds. He had only one individual stock holding—tobacco giant Altria, formerly known as Philip Morris.

It's easy to understand why. In his 2005 book, *The Future for Investors*, Wharton professor Jeremy Siegel found that Altria was the most profitable stock investment in U.S. history.

A thousand dollars invested in the S&P 500 at its inception in 1957 would have grown, with dividends reinvested, to $125,000 by the time of Siegel's publishing. Not bad. **But $1,000 invested in Altria (then Philip Morris) would have grown to *$4.6 million*.** Siegel writes,

> Philip Morris's outstanding performance does not just date from mid-century. Philip Morris was also the best-performing company since 1925, the date when comprehensive returns on individual stocks were first compiled. From the end of 1925 though the end of 2003, Philip Morris delivered a 17 percent compound annual return, 7.3 percent greater than the market indexes. An initial $1,000 invested in this firm in 1925, with dividends reinvested, would now be worth ***over a quarter of a billion dollars!***

Not a bad run indeed.

I can already hear what you're thinking, though: "You're relying too heavily on historical information. Those stats were before the era of class action lawsuits."

Well, the numbers don't lie. The tobacco lawsuits started in earnest in 1996. Let's take a look at how Altria did compared to the S&P 500 using that date as the start point:

- Total return on Altria, 1996–present: **499%**
- Total return on the S&P 500, 1996–present: **130%**

**During one of the most difficult environments in the industry's history, Altria managed to outperform the market by 369 percent!**

In fact, the periodic price drops actually *helped* Altria's performance over the long term. If you are reinvesting your quarterly dividends, you are thrilled if the share price takes a temporary nose dive prior to the payment. A lower share prices means that your reinvested dividend funds can buy more shares, which begets more future dividends and allows your investment to compound at a faster rate. Assuming that the price volatility is not due to some kind of permanent impairment to the business, a lower price (and thus higher dividend yield) is a blessing.

Reaching a similar conclusion as James Montier, Siegel found that over the long term, **97% of inflation-adjusted stock returns comes from the reinvestment of dividends**. Only three percent comes from capital gains.

We may or may not see returns like this going forward; only time will tell. But Dr. Siegel's point is well made. The reinvestment of dividends can turn mediocre returns into phenomenal returns over time, and good returns into mind-boggling returns. So, unless you need the income today for current living expenses, **follow Dr. Siegel's advice and reinvest your dividends**. Many stock brokers offer this service for free, on request.

# Chapter 13:

# Where Not to Invest

I am generally an optimist, and I like to focus on the positive. Frankly, I find this to be a far healthier and more profitable way to live my life. Nearly all successful people are at heart optimists, almost to a fault. If you think about it, you would *have* to be an optimist to start a business or to be successful in your career. Those with negative or fatalistic attitudes tend to not go very far in life.

So, it is natural that I tend to focus on what investments I think will do well in the years ahead instead of focusing on what investments I think will do poorly. But I think it is also important to mention assets I think you should specifically avoid. After all, the best way to win in investing is to avoid losing. One bad bear market can reverse years or even decades of steady gains. We all know that investors with large positions in tech stocks in 2000 or financial stocks in 2008 would have been a lot better off had they avoided those unfortunate sectors.

I'll start with one of the most popular investments of the 2000s: **gold**. As the 1990s tech bubble was collapsing, gold seemed like a pretty good alternative to stocks. It helped that gold had been in a 20-year bear market and that it was selling for less than $300 per ounce. No one wanted anything to do with gold, making the "barbarous relic" the perfect contrarian investment.

That was then. This is now. More than a decade into a raging bull market, the price of gold has soared from less than $300 per ounce to over $1,400. While I understand the philosophical arguments for gold—it's a hedge against currency debasement, inflation, instability, etc.—at $1,400 per ounce, you really have to ask yourself if all of these fears are already factored into the price. Let's say that, despite my predictions to the contrary, we do get a surge of inflation. Haven't investors already pushed up the gold price in anticipation? Exactly how high would inflation have to get for gold to rise significantly from current levels?

Of course, this is an impossible question to answer because gold is an impossible asset to value. It is debatable whether gold is really an asset at all. It has no earnings and doesn't pay income in the form of dividends or interest. With stocks, you can get a rough idea of what a stock is worth by comparing its market price to its earnings, dividends or book value. But how do you do this with gold? It's an inanimate blob of yellow metal!

Something I find a little disturbing is how politicized the gold bugs have become. To a large vocal minority of the gold buying population, gold is not just an investment. It's a political ideology based on an intense loathing of the government, and of the Federal Reserve in particular, fueled by an antiestablishment angst that I haven't seen since the 1970s.

Don't get me wrong, I think governments are out of control and I often question the wisdom of the Federal Reserve. But smart investors don't let their political views affect their investment decision making. We can whine and moan about the Fed's creation of bubbles, or we can position our portfolios accordingly and actually make money. Hey, there is a lot to be angry about these days. But frankly, I prefer to be an optimist. It's a lot easier to make money that way.

To determine the value of gold, you cannot say with any certainty whether it is overpriced or underpriced. Instead, you have to rely on sentiment and anecdotal evidence. Let's pick apart some of the gold bug arguments.

Many of the gold bug assumptions fall flat in the face of critical analysis. If inflation and dollar depreciation are such significant threats, then why are we not seeing higher yields in the bond market? Yes, at time of writing, yields were rising—modestly. They are still near all-time lows, however. If the Federal Reserve is somehow preventing yields from rising due to its open market operations, then why would they allow gold to rise when they could just as easily manipulate its price as well via the futures market?

But most fundamentally, the gold bugs fail to answer one important question: *why is gold valuable?* The gold bug answer is that it is protection from the abuses of fiat currencies (i.e., ones with value only through government regulation or law) but as Richard Wiggins stated in a *Barron's* article, *gold* is *a fiat currency.*

Gold is valuable because we all agree it's valuable, and new supplies are mined daily. How is this different from the dollar or the euro? More than calling it a fiat currency, Brett Arends goes so far as to call gold a "Ponzi scheme" in a recent *Wall Street Journal* article.

He makes a good point. Unlike most other commodities, it has no significant intrinsic value, as its industrial uses are in decline. The only way to make money in gold is to find someone else to buy your gold at a higher price. This works only so long as there are more and more new investors. Come to think of it, that *does* sound a bit like a Ponzi scheme.

Most disturbingly, I see some major divergences in the buying patterns of investors and consumers of gold. In 2009, demand for gold as an investment exceeded demand for gold as jewelry for the first time since 1980—*which happened to be the year that the last bull market in gold collapsed.*

But perhaps more telling are the recent numbers out of India. India has been the world's biggest consumer of gold since time immemorial. But Indian gold consumption has actually been in decline since 2005 (see Figure 13.1)—this during a period in which India enjoyed an economic boom and incomes rose substantially among the middle and upper classes.

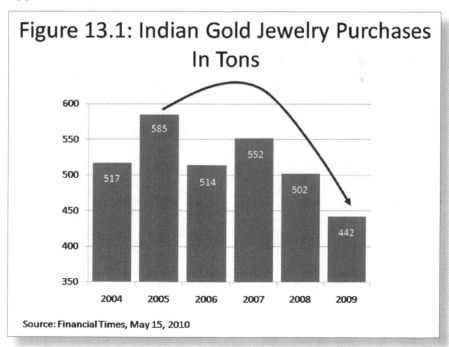

Figure 13.1: Indian Gold Jewelry Purchases In Tons

Source: Financial Times, May 15, 2010

Here's another example that will blow your mind. With gold becoming unaffordable for many young couples, jewelers had started selling new "precious" metals such as tungsten and titanium for use as wedding rings.

Titanium? This is a metal that is used to make golf clubs, and it's being advertised as a precious metal because the average groom has now been priced out of the market for traditional precious metals like gold and platinum.

But perhaps the most absurd anecdote yet comes from the Middle East. In Abu Dhabi, you can now get one-ounce Krugerrand coins out of an ATM machine! This is madness. Gold's traditional uses are all in decline, while the price surges due to new interest from retail investors ordering coins from late-night infomercials. It would appear that gold is being transferred from the informed "smart" money to the uninformed "dumb" money.

It's impossible to know exactly when or how this bubble will end. It's clear to me that it is primarily being used as a third currency in the face of countries continuing to print money and therefore debasing their currencies. But when does this come screeching to a halt?

Writing for the *Financial Times*, James Mackintosh suggests that gold is leaving the boom stage and is now entering the euphoria stage—that last surge before the inevitable bust. The natural course of action would be to sell gold short, but this is far easier said than done. As John Maynard Keynes famously said, "the market can stay irrational longer than you can stay solvent."

Mackintosh reckons that gold could double or even quadruple before eventually collapsing, if history is any guide. We shall certainly see. But in any event, gold should be viewed with skepticism as an investment at this point, although I do like it as a possible hedge against a calamity. At the very least, use the recent strength as an opportunity to rebalance your portfolio, keeping gold and precious metals to a prudent allocation and avoid getting caught up in the hype to over-allocate.

I'll end this diatribe on gold with a little insight from Warren Buffett. The Oracle of Omaha once said *"Gold gets dug out of the ground in Africa, or someplace. Then we melt it down, dig another hole, bury it again and pay people to stand around guarding it. It has no utility. Anyone watching from Mars would be scratching their head."*

Gold is the highest-profile "hard" asset these days, but it's certainly not alone in its popularity. Commodities in general have had a great run over the past decade. With the global economy showing signs of recovery, there is renewed talk that demand from China and India will keep commodity prices high and rising for decades to come.

Really? Whenever I hear these kinds of arguments, I cringe a little. This is bad analysis. These same conditions were equally true ten years ago, when prices were at multi-decade lows. As economies grow and mature, they do initially use more commodities, particularly energy. But they also become far more efficient in their use of commodities. Rising prices give them no other choice. Fuel efficiency is much higher today than in years past. With home heating and air conditioning prices as high as they are, homes are becoming more efficient, as are appliances.

The same is true of manufacturing processes. Consider the case of automobiles. Cars today use a lot less metal than they used to, having replaced it with cheaper, lighter materials. This is true of homes too, for that matter. Given how low incomes are in India and China, is it plausible that Indian and Chinese consumers and businesses will pay any price for the materials they need? I think not.

But while consumers seem to get this and respond to higher prices by curtailing their consumption, investors appear to be clueless. As Peter Tasker put it in a *Financial Times* editorial,

> Di-*worse*-ification is what you do when you invest in mediocre assets for a mediocre reason—for example, because a statistical model has told you they reduce risk. Thanks to the boom in commodities during the past decade, these have become a favored choice for di-worse-ifying institutions everywhere. The profusion of funds and exchange-traded funds, indices and brokerage coverage has made commodities unprecedentedly easy to access for individuals too. However, the long-term performance of commodities is pathetic, and there is little reason to believe that this time is different[32].

Investors who piled into commodities at the end of the 1970s regretted it, and investors who are piling in today are unlikely to fare much better. In fact, there is a good case to be made that it is the investors themselves who are forcing prices up. Many commodities are currently priced in "contango." Essentially, that means when too many investors try to buy the same futures contract at the same time, it forces up the price of that contract relative to longer-dated contracts on the same commodity. So, passive commodity investors who "roll over" their contracts on expiration get absolutely screwed. They buy the front-month contract high and sell it low… over and over again. If the spot price is in a strong uptrend and the contango is only mild, you might not notice. But if the market is flat or only mildly rising, you can actually lose a lot of money as the negative roll yield grinds away at the value of your account every month.

Most of the popular new mutual funds and ETFs that track commodities suffer from this problem, and I'd be willing to bet a large sum of money that the investors buying these products have no idea this is the case.

Investors must also be conscious of the fact that quantitative easing by the Fed does create higher commodity prices through a lower dollar. It's like an artificial sweetener. Commodities are priced in dollars, so as the dollar goes down, commodity prices go up and imports cost more for the same reason. A lower dollar makes import prices rise.

Now, I do sometimes use gold and silver in portfolios for different reasons, when I believe the pricing to be favorable. At the right price, precious metals can be effective as a currency or an apocalypse hedge. However, in general, it is best to leave commodities to the commodities traders who understand things like contango. There are other, better ways for us to make money.

I'll wrap this up with another humorous quote from Mr. Tasker:

> Commodities don't *deserve* to generate any return. As the name suggests, they are undifferentiated lumps of naturally occurring materials. Value needs to be added to them by the application of knowledge; it is investment in that process of application that earns the return. Over the long haul the price of the commodities themselves reverts to the cost of production.
>
> As societies become more sophisticated, knowledge generates ever greater returns. By contrast, societies in which commodities are highly valued are by definition primitive. That is why the price of copper peaked out in ancient Egyptian times, when a few kilograms could buy you a slave girl. Its purchasing power has been in decline ever since. *In essence copper has been in a bear market for 3,000 years.* Consider that before you di-*worse*-ify.

# Conclusion

We've come a long way from those fateful days at the Arenal lodge in Costa Rica when the meteor—just seconds from impact—narrowly avoided earth. Since the market bottom in March 2009, stocks have soared, and the pain and hysteria that investors felt during that volatile period seems like a distant memory. Even some of the highest-profile casualties—such as General Motors—have been brought back from the dead. It's as if the crisis never happened. Life appears to be returning to normal... so far, that is. People's memories are much too short.

The government tells us that everything has been fixed and we are on the road to recovery, but I'm not buying it. The meltdown and crisis of 2008 was caused by excessive debts in the financial and mortgage sectors. And while debt levels are slowly falling in these areas, government debt has exploded in response. I cannot imagine that years from now, when we look back on this period, the solution was to just print money and throw it into the economy without getting to the root of the problem: having too much debt to begin with!

There is no doubt that America is at a crossroads. The government may try to convince us that the crisis is over, but we're only half way through at best. Economic fundamentals, market cycles and demographic trends are all converging in such a way that threatens the long term prosperity to which we Americans have become accustomed. The combination of Baby Boomers passing their peak spending years, an enormously over indebted consumer and a government in crisis over how to pay for entitlement programs is brewing up a storm of epic proportions, and it will affect the way you live and invest.

We've just gone through 20+ years of a borrowing and spending binge, and a massive wave of deleveraging is happening as a result. We had a great party; unfortunately, it left a killer hangover that we now have to suffer through.

The factors that make the spending spree of the 1990s and 2000s possible will not be repeated in the years ahead. Those Baby Boomers that fueled the boom in their early middle age are now past their peak spending years. Rather than act as gasoline on the economic fire, they will now act as a wet blanket. The next decade will see these Boomers saving every penny they can, and a penny saved is distinctly *not* a penny spent in the economy.

The second factor was easy lending. When the Boomers—and the rest of the country too, for that matter—ran out of money to spend, they simply borrowed more. With home prices rising and interest rates low, it was easy to extract equity from their homes. But with home prices stagnant and actually still falling in several major markets there is very little equity left to extract. And even if there was, the battered banks are in very poor position to make loans. The same is true of credit card companies, auto finance companies, and anyone else who traditionally lends money to consumers.

And the government? With the budget deficit at record levels, the national debt spiraling out of control and the enormous Social Security and Medicare expenditures coming down the pipeline, how exactly is the government going to be in a position to help with any of this? You can be certain that it won't be.

Now, we as a country must pay the tab for spending more than we made. This reduction in borrowing and spending and increase in saving and paying down debts is deflationary. While we may see pockets of inflation here or there due to the Fed's monetary stimulus, history suggests that it is deflation we can look forward to in the years ahead.

As we speak, Fed Chairman Ben Bernanke and his financial puppeteers are printing money like mad to keep the economy afloat and ahead of inevitable deflation. This is not so much fixing the economy as it is repairing the bank's balance sheets in preparation for the next wave. Unemployment is astronomically high (even Ben Bernanke admits it will take at least five years to bring it down), housing is in a veritable depression and not likely to recover for four or five years, and people won't buy more stuff (mostly stuff they don't need anyway, but that's the American way) because they are already leveraged to the hilt.

The government response has given us a federal budget deficit that would rival a banana republic, mortgaging our children's future (sorry Josh), on the cheap. It's nothing more than a giant Ponzi scheme. The sad part is that it has had little net effect on the economy because private sector deleveraging is more than offsetting the government stimulus. In simple terms, assets are shrinking faster than the government can inflate them.

Yet the stock market continues to rise, largely because economic indicators are being perverted more than at any time in our lifetimes by the unprecedented government stimulus programs which are slowing down the natural deleveraging process that needs to happen if we are to return to health. Unfortunately, all we are doing is creating another bubble, and we all know what happens to bubbles… they burst, and when they burst, it's ugly.

Armed with the information in this book, you can not only survive the most dangerous market in a generation, but you could be one of the few that prosper. Few saw Goliath rolling up his sleeves last time and the next will be no different. However, those that are prepared will flourish, while those that are not will endure tremendous financial and personal hardship. Your financial well-being and ultimately your way of life depend on you being properly equipped to face the Goliath that stands before you.

# Appendix A: An Economic Tsunami Lies Ahead—Prepare For This Perfect Storm; Your Way of Life Depends on It!

*This section was originally published as a special report to Springer Financial Advisors clients in December of 2007—well before the onset of the 2008 crisis and meltdown. The original charts have been removed because they have already been discussed at length in the main body of the book.*

America is at a crossroads. The convergence of economic fundamentals, market cycles and demographic trends threatens the long-term economic prosperity to which we Americans have become accustomed. With Baby Boomers passing their peak spending years, a record number of Americans retiring and a government in crisis over how to pay for it, a storm of epic proportions is brewing. Few will see it coming, but those who are prepared may prosper, while those who are not will endure tremendous financial and personal hardship. Your financial well-being and ultimately your way of life depend on being ready for this Perfect Storm, this Economic Tsunami.

Soon, the 78 million Baby Boomers will pass their peak spending years and head into retirement. It's an important time because America is a nation driven by consumer spending. Personal consumption, or what people do as consumers, represents over 70% of the nation's Gross Domestic Product (GDP) and consumer spending is the largest factor in our economic health. Boom times are associated with an increasing size of the mid-forties population, because this is the age people spend the most, and bust times are associated with a decreasing size of this population. As larger groups of consumers reach an age when they spend more, the economy grows. In turn, when these groups pass their peak spending years, the economy slows—dramatically.

People spend money in predictable patterns at predictable times in their lives. These spending patterns directly impact our economy, business and product trends. They affect everything from the demand for potato chips and real estate to inflation rates, economic growth, immigration rates and domestic migration. By analyzing this information we can forecast how spending will change in the years and decades to come. Economists will continue to fret about the "over-extended" consumers and the dire consequences to come, however the boom in consumer spending will continue until Baby Boomers see their children finish their high school years and move out. How do we know all this? Demographics!

Demographics—The Ultimate Forecasting Tool

Demographic data categorizes consumers by age, income, lifestyles— even zip codes and neighborhood blocks. It predicts what new generations of consumers will do as they age, and it can help us see key trends that will affect our future. The life insurance industry was the first to use this data for actuarial predictions and risk assessment.

An economic boom is not just created by the rise of spending (demand), but also the simultaneous rise of productivity (supply) from an efficient maturing generation. This generates rising stock prices from higher earnings and rising valuations, along with low inflation. When older people leave the workforce, they are replaced with a younger, less efficient workforce, which leads to decreasing productivity with increasing inflation. The next cycle occurs once the spenders are gone, leading to decreasing prices for goods and services causing deflation.

People do predictable things as they age. Between ages 18 and 47, we go through several stages of life. From just entering the workforce at ages 18 to 22, and getting married between ages 22 and 30, the spending cycle is accelerated. Once children enter the picture, we typically then purchase our first home between ages 31 and 42. This is the stage at which we incur the most debt—and buy the most potato chips for ravenous 14-year-olds. Our spending continues to increase as we purchase our next home, more furnishings and cars, etc., until about age 47, as our kids reach their late teenage years and are still living in the household.

As we reach 50, the kids leave home. At this point, apart from that dream car at 54 and the expensive wine at 56, we begin to spend less, pay down debts and save more for retirement. Income doesn't decrease, but investment usually does. The peak rate of investment generally occurs at age 54, which continues into retirement at around age 63. Net worth typically peaks just after age of death, currently 78. With quantifiable data on all of the key things we do as we age, trends are largely predictable decades into the future.

Consider the events that looked like they would seriously derail the economy, but didn't—September 11, Hurricane Katrina and the Afghanistan and Iraq Wars, to name a few. How did we go through these incredible obstacles and yet spend more? These disasters and threats are not what we base our spending decisions on. Families have needs that must be taken care of regardless of the current market conditions. As we move through stages of life, we change our spending in very predictable ways. To better understand these dynamics, we must look at the Adjusted Birth Index.

Spending cycles can be forecasted by moving forward the birth index (adjusted for immigration) by the appropriate number of years to correlate with the size of the late forties population. If we plot the size of the late forties age group with the projected year, we see the rising trend of peaks and troughs in spending due to past variations in birth and immigration rates. For example, fewer babies were born during the Great Depression. Thus, we would expect that 48 years later (during the 1970's) there would be fewer middle-aged people, thus the stagnation of the 1970's economy. Generation X (the Baby Boomers' children) are barely 1/3 the size of the Baby Boomer generation (1946-1964). From this we bear witness to a very alarming fact; there just physically are not enough people in Generation X to keep up the pace of spending set by the Baby Boomers!

When the massive Baby Boomer generation finally passes its peak spending years, spending will slow, earnings will decline and stock valuations will fall dramatically. We have already seen this effect on real estate, which likely will not rebound until 2012-2015 when the Echo Boomers begin to buy their first homes. There are just not enough people to absorb the homes of the current generation. To make matters even worse, retiring boomers will be living off of their assets and subsequently selling assets in a declining market, forcing them to sell more to just to get the same amount of money. Add in a Social Security and Medicare system stretched beyond their breaking points to service this swell of retirees, and the government will be forced to raise taxes regardless of who is in the White House... A perfect storm.

Why does this matter?

In managing your finances, it is important to have a reasonable idea of what your expenses will be, especially in retirement. How will economic and demographic trends and inflation affect those expenses? A financial plan that assumes rising consumer prices will look very different from one that assumes stagnant or falling prices. A portfolio of bonds and cash would be decimated by a period of prolonged inflation, but it would be very profitable during a deflationary period. On the other hand, a portfolio of stocks and commodities should do relatively well in keeping pace with inflation but would be catastrophic during a period of deflation. Naturally, having a viable economic forecast that takes these factors into account is an essential part of building your financial plan.

The single most important financial decision you will make in the next ten years will be your money management style and the asset allocation you choose as economic cycles shift. Choose well and you will be able to enjoy the products and services you buy at a lower cost, while watching your nest egg grow. Choose poorly and your nest egg will shrink and you will see your purchasing power erode. In the ensuing bear market, millions of Americans will lose their life savings—don't be one of them.

In Conclusion

As my longtime clients will attest, I am not a doom and gloom pessimist or a non-believer in the American way. To the contrary, I have been bullish for most of my 25+ years in the industry. I believe America is the greatest nation the world has ever known, and there is nothing in our future we cannot overcome. Naturally, I hope my predictions are wrong, but we simply cannot take that chance and not be prepared. The media would have you believe that headlines move markets, and nobody knows what is going to be the next "most-important-thing-ever" to the media. What I do know is that, as powerful as wars, hurricanes and oil spikes might be, the spending cycle will continue to dominate the economy. When the Baby Boom ends, it will be vital to your way of life that you know how to invest to protect yourself and your family—and to profit. Regardless of the economic conditions, I will be ready for my clients.

# About Keith Springer

Keith Springer began his career in 1985 at Merrill Lynch in his hometown of Boston, Massachusetts. In 1990, he tired of shoveling snow and moved to sunny California to study advanced portfolio management and investment management studies. In 1996, he became an independent Registered Investment Advisor and formed Springer Financial Advisors (formerly Capital Financial Advisory Services) where he continues to serve as president today. He regularly appears as an analyst on a variety of national financial news outlets including *CNBC, Fox Business, The Wall Street Journal, The New York Times* and many others. Keith Springer lives in Sacramento with his son Josh.

# Notes

1. Paul McCulley, "The Liquidity Conundrum" *CFA Institute Conference Proceedings Quarterly*, March 2008.
2. The role of the velocity can be best understood by looking at the Equation of Exchange, an integral part of the Quantity Theory of Money beloved by the monetarist school of thought:

   $$MV_T = P_T T \text{ where}$$

   M = money supply
   $V_T$ = velocity of money
   $P_T$ = price level at time T
   T = aggregate real value of all transactions for the period

   For a longer explanation, see http://en.wikipedia.org/wiki/Quantity_theory_of_money.
3. Bill Bonner and Addison Wiggin, *Financial Reckoning Day*, 2003
4. See Biblical book of Ecclesiastes.
5. Reinhart and Rogoff also authored an academic paper by the same name that covers much of the same material, available for free on the Harvard Economics Department website: http://www.economics.harvard.edu/files/faculty/51_This_Time_Is_Different.pdf.
6. See http://en.wikipedia.org/wiki/Strauss_and_Howe for a good summary of their work.
7. See http://en.wikipedia.org/wiki/Hyman_Minsky#Understanding_Minsky.27s_Financial_Instability_Hypothesis.

8.  See Reinhart, Carmen M. and Kenneth S. Rogoff (2010). "Growth in a Time of Debt," *American Economic Review,* Vol. 100 No. 2, May 2010, 573-78.
9.  http://terpconnect.umd.edu/~creinhar/Papers/RR%20 Debt%20and%20Growth-01-18%20NBER.pdf.
10. Ferguson, Niall. "Complexity and Collapse: Empires on the Edge of Chaos." *Foreign Affairs*, March/April 2010.
11. For a well-written account in digestible modern English, I recommend *Financial Reckoning Day* by William Bonner and Addison Wiggin (which was recently republished). Bonner and Wiggin devote an entire chapter to Law's scheme, and many of the precise figures used in this chapter were taken from their book.

    For a longer account of the John Law fiasco, I recommend *Extraordinary Popular Delusions and the Madness of Crowds* by Charles Mackey.

    Niall Ferguson, in his *Ascent of Money*, also gives a good telling of the unfortunate story.

12. The Five Stages were quoted directly from Niall Ferguson's *The Ascent of Money*, but Ferguson's original source was Charles Kindleberger's *Manias, Panics, and Crashes*, which was in turn largely based on the pioneering work of Hyman Minsky. I highly recommend all three authors.
13. From *The Wealth of Nations*, Book IV.
14. "Say's Law" is attributed to Jean-Baptiste Say (1767-1832), the noted French classical economist, and is a standard tenet of several schools of economic thought, including classical, neo-classical, supply-side, and Austrian.
15. DellaVigna and Pollet's paper is available at the University of California at Berkley website: http://www.econ.berkeley.edu/~sdellavi/wp/attention.pdf.
16. See Birchall, Jonathan. "Two Men and a Baby Business," *Financial Times*, April 6, 2010 http://www.ft.com/cms/s/0/17d97d70-41b3-11df-865a-00144feabdc0.html.

17. See Simon, Bernard. "U.S. motorcycle sector extends decline." *Financial Times*, October 24, 2010 http://www.ft.com/cms/s/0/653c974c-df9b-11df-bed9-00144feabdc0.html.

18. See "Oktobergloom," *The Economist*, October 7, 2010 http://www.economist.com/node/17204871.

19. See Pignal, Stanley. "Dutch look at weeding out cannabis cafes," *Financial Times*, October 8, 2010 http://www.ft.com/cms/s/0/2cc0e802-d2fb-11df-9ae9-00144feabdc0.html.

20. Timothy Cogley and Heather Royer. "The Baby Boom, the Baby Bust, and Asset Markets," Federal Reserve Board of San Francisco Economic Letter, June 26, 1998.

21. Levy, Leon. *The Mind of Wall Street: A Legendary Financier on the Perils of Greed and the Mysteries of the Market*, 2002.

22. Haberman, Clyde, "People behaving poorly may be the ones to save the state from the poorhouse," *New York Times*, December 2008.

23. Robbins, Gary. Estate taxes: An historical perspective, *Backgrounder*, January 16, 2004.

24. Hyman, David A. *Medicare Meets Mephistopheles*. New York: The Cato Institute, 2006.

25. Swerlick, Robert A. "Our Soviet Health System." *Wall Street Journal*, June 5, 2007.

26. "Sicko" *Forbes*, August 13, 2007.

27. Pauly, Mark V. "The Economics of Moral Hazard." *The American Economic Review*, Vol. 58, No. 3, Part 1 (Jun., 1968), pp. 531-537.

28. Havighurst, Clark C. *Health Care Choices*. Washington, DC: The AEI Press, 1995.

29. For a general description of the LTCM story, see Lowenstein, Roger. *When Genius Failed*. Random House, 2003.

30. Kolman, Joel. "LTCM Speaks." www.derivativesstrategy.com.

31. Taleb, Nassim Nicholas. *The Black Swan*. Random House, 2007.

32. Montier, James. "Was It All Just A Bad Dream?" February 2010 GMO White Paper.

33. Tasker, Peter. "Why The Bulls Have Got It All Wrong With Commodities," *Financial Times*, June 10, 2010.